NORTHERN
VERMONT
in the
REVOLUTIONARY WAR

NORTHERN
VERMONT
in the
REVOLUTIONARY WAR

JASON BARNEY

THE
History
PRESS

Published by The History Press
Charleston, SC
www.historypress.com

Front cover: The Gundalow *Boston* off the coast of Isle La Motte and Alburgh in the late summer and fall of 1776. This vessel was part of Benedict Arnold's fleet as it desperately attempted to fight off the British invasion from Quebec. *James A. Flood of James A. Flood Maritime Art Inc.*
Back cover, top: Library of Congress; *bottom*: photograph by the author.

First published 2022

Manufactured in the United States

ISBN 9781467150040

Library of Congress Control Number: 2022933366

Notice: The information in this book is true and complete to the best of our knowledge. It is offered without guarantee on the part of the author or The History Press. The author and The History Press disclaim all liability in connection with the use of this book.

For Samuel Barney, the best son a father could have.

CONTENTS

ACKNOWLEDGEMENTS

I would like to thank my friends and colleagues at Missisquoi Valley Union High School for tolerating my attempts to associate everything with local history. Special thanks go out to Jay Hartman, Dan Palmer, Alyssa Urban and Jenn Desorgher, for your continuing faith in me. I would like to acknowledge all of the young learners at the school and hope the time you spend in my classes is worth it.

Lindsay Didio, Ashley Bowen, Josh Sinz and Armand Messier…thank you so much for contributing your artistic talents. Your abilities add so much to the books.

Definite positive thoughts to the Vermont Archaeological Society and its efforts to bring its area of study to the classroom. Specifically, the Freedom and Unity National Endowment of the Humanities grant I was involved with during the summer of 2021 was an incredible experience.

Thanks to the Barney family, for all of your support and interest.

I would like to thank my wife, Christine, who energetically supports my writing and is always there for me. She reads these works before they are sent off to the editor and makes very insightful suggestions. She supports my research and is a talented researcher herself. Chris, thanks for everything.

Thanks go out to my son, Sam, who has also fallen in love with reading and writing.

To Mike Kinsella and The History Press, thanks for giving me these opportunities.

To you, dear reader, thank you for wanting more.

YOUR HOME, YOUR HISTORY

It has been a few years since *Northern Vermont in the War of 1812* was published. That project started when I researched the historical treasures of my home area.

I can't stop myself from doing research. That my home has a well-chronicled but somewhat forgotten military history is just fascinating.

Our place in the world is not defined by our present small-town reality. Quite the opposite. Swanton, Alburgh, Highgate, Isle La Motte and the nearby areas of Lake Champlain were places where armies camped and navies anchored.

My next book, *The Hidden History of Franklin County*, went a little beyond military happenings. It explored the vast swath of events and people that inhabited this region since the first indigenous peoples. It covered interesting topics, from Prohibition to the counterculture.

And now you are reading my third book. I am honored to have put this one together.

Everyone knows something about the American Revolution. Even the laziest citizens remember something about George Washington, Ben Franklin or Benedict Arnold. They know that British soldiers wore bright red uniforms. They are aware of the struggle that led to the birth of the United States.

It started near Boston. The "shots heard around the world" were at Lexington and Concord.

What happened here in the Champlain Valley is part of that story.

Benedict Arnold, Ethan Allen and the Green Mountain Boys took Fort Ticonderoga. In our backyard.

That is not all, however.

Many historians have only touched on the valuable and important local veins of history in the broader context of well-known events. A colonial army sailed north on Lake Champlain and invaded Quebec. They took Montreal and linked up with Benedict Arnold's army moving north through Maine, then laid siege to Quebec. That effort failed, and the next year, Americans were in full retreat throughout the Champlain Valley.

In 1777, there was a British offensive meant to end the war. Ticonderoga fell to the enemy. The Battle of Hubbardton, the only major conflict to happen in Vermont, played out in July. The Battle of Bennington was next, followed by the British defeat at Saratoga. It's all in the history books, page after page of major events.

What has not been analyzed, at least in any great detail, is how northern Vermont was heavily involved with all of these events. Colonial spies snuck through the woods of Highgate and Swanton to find out what the British were up to in Canada. While engaged in various missions, Benedict Arnold, Ethan Allen and Ben Franklin were on ships on bodies of water where many of us fish, swim and relax. The towns of Grand Isle, North Hero, South Hero, Isle La Motte and Alburgh have unique Revolutionary War histories.

Like whispered secrets, many people don't know about the American blockhouses on the Onion River in Winooski, or the military road constructed from the Connecticut River all the way to Franklin County. Conventional history does not go into much detail about Île aux Noix, the British military installation just a few miles north of Missisquoi Bay. The raids, retreats and scouting missions through Missisquoi Bay are so obscure in the larger history that they generally aren't even footnoted among the "greater" events in popular texts.

Until now.

I cannot describe the joy and excitement I experienced when I realized the region in which I grew up was directly related to critically important historical events.

I am interested in the circumstances of people in times of conflict. The sacrifice by everyday soldiers was truly remarkable. The physical toll was more than most would want to experience. The emotional and psychological scarring was also immense. Post-traumatic stress, bodily harm and death are all wrapped up in the idea of fighting for one's ideals, and patriotic individuals do step forward. This book explores this patriotism and the other reasons why people came to the Champlain Valley to fight a war.

A more in-depth exploration of different perspectives of the past can give us a better understanding of what happened in the places where we live, plant our gardens and visit with neighbors.

The coming pages will try to weave economic, social and military history into something northern Vermonters can be proud of. Contrary to what most people think, a lot of history unfolded up here in our little corner of the world, and surprisingly, not much is known about it.

I would like to share it with you.

A BRIEF NOTE ABOUT geography: In the coming pages, you will read much about "Prattsburgh." You will not find this location on any present-day maps. It is not the same location as Plattsburgh, New York. Plattsburgh is on the western shore of Lake Champlain and does not receive much attention in this story.

Prattsburgh was the original name of Swanton, Vermont. It was first surveyed by New Yorkers. The name *Swanton* was adopted during the period of the Revolution and is associated with the New Hampshire Grants and Benning Wentworth.

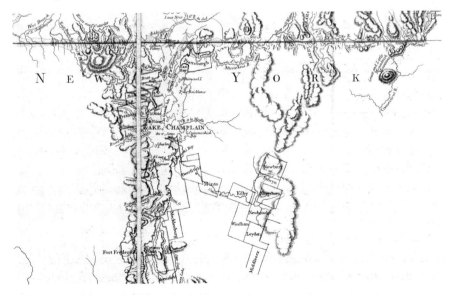

Early maps of Vermont from the late 1700s have Swanton listed by its original name, Prattsburgh. *Courtesy of the Library of Congress.*

Chapter 1

MORE THAN A CENTURY OF WAR,
A DECADE OF PEACE

During the French and Indian War, the Champlain Valley hosted intense fighting. Those events are linked to the long military history of the region, which involved the French in Quebec and the English in New England continuously battling each other. Each colonial force was secure in its own part of the continent, but when they started to explore outward, the wars that ravaged Europe found their way here. Native American tribes were wrapped up in a struggle that was not theirs but that unfolded in their homelands.

When the last of those wars ended, the seeds for the struggle of American independence had already been sown. By the late 1700s, many people in the English colonies were subjects of the Crown but were born an ocean away from the throne. If the average English resident wanted to leave their country behind, imagine the questions and frustrations of those born into freedom, never experiencing life in the homeland. Feelings of resentment, irritation and independence were a natural result of living thousands of miles from England. Following the French and Indian War, colonials wondered why British soldiers were still around.

Those feelings were shaped by a long history of European colonialism.

The fighting started when the French claimed the St. Lawrence River in Quebec. England and other countries had already staked a claim to the Atlantic coast.

Samuel Champlain established Quebec City and Montreal in the early 1600s. In 1609, he ventured through the shallow waters of the Richelieu

River, moving south into Lake Champlain. He was allied with the Algonquin tribes and confronted the Iroquois with his guns. The skirmish aligned the aggressive Iroquois Confederacy with the English colonies to the south, setting up the alliances that defined the French and Indian War.

Conflict came to define the region. The French constructed forts as far south as Isle La Motte in 1666. Fort St. Anne didn't last long but was a major installation in the effort to keep the Iroquois at arm's length. To the south, the English were also having trouble with French-allied tribes, and King Philip's War exploded across New England in 1675. A decade later, King William's War raged. Military campaigns were carried out all over the Northeast, including in the Champlain Valley. Then came Queen Anne's War. Water routes provided quick and efficient movement of armies, and Lake Champlain allowed both sides to deposit military units on the enemy's doorstep. Whoever controlled Lake Champlain controlled the region.

In the early 1730s, the French constructed Fort St. Frederic, which allowed them to control the Champlain Valley. It helped defend Quebec, especially when King George's War erupted in the 1740s. French colonists, looking to establish a comfortable foothold over the land, developed the region.

France understood that its toehold in North America was precarious, so it constructed Fort Carillon even farther south than Fort St. Frederic. France now had two massive military installations on Lake Champlain to defend Quebec. However, they had a much smaller population in North America than did the British. When the French and Indian War erupted in the mid-1750s, the French army was in a difficult position. French Canadians were vastly outnumbered by the British pushing into the Champlain Valley. Soon, the two fortresses were under British control. Carillon was renamed Fort Ticonderoga. Fort St. Frederic was named Crown Point, and the British dominated the region. The French still had small settlements in the northern areas of the lake and prepared a desperate defense by fortifying the island of Île aux Noix, just north of Missisquoi Bay. British forces soon swept over the lake and conquered Montreal and Quebec City. From that point, France's North American possessions became part of the English empire. English American settlers moved into territory in the early 1760s.

Now that England dominated the continent, its own colonies competed for the newly available lands.

New Hampshire, which had a small coastline on the Atlantic, wanted to expand north and west, stretching its border beyond the Connecticut River. New York, tucked into a small area on the Atlantic, believed it had the right to expand north and east, beyond the Hudson River Valley. In between were the Green Mountains, stretching from the northern boundary of Massachusetts to the as yet undefined border with Quebec. Colonists from both sides descended on the land.

At this early stage, some of Vermont's "Founding Fathers" were forced to acknowledge that New York had already set up legitimate areas of government as far east as the Connecticut River.[1] However, the settlers from New Hampshire thought the land was ripe for the taking. As early as 1761, Governor Benning Wentworth pushed his colony's claim and granted as many as sixty new townships in the Green Mountains.[2] For them, the land was called the "New Hampshire Grants."

New York's claim, especially around Lake Champlain, was linked to the war that had just ended. Significant British forces had moved up the Hudson River valley, and New York had developed settlements near Lake George. The English government wanted the British army to work with New York colonial officials.[3] Recent scholarship has documented that war veterans believed an entirely separate colony from New York and New Hampshire could be created. While the matter remained unsettled, New York and the British military had approximately eight hundred laborers at Crown Point in 1761. In a real application of the principle that "possession is nine-tenths of the law," they were gardening the land and repairing the fort.

Tense encounters between New York and New Hampshire occurred as early as 1762. New Hampshire officials arrived across from Crown Point, believing the land was theirs to survey and sell. Just a few months later, in 1763, Benning Wentworth further complicated the situation when he granted another thirty-seven towns. Many were on the edge of territory that New Yorkers were interested in, generally along the Onion River, today's Winooski River. Some of these claims, including Swanton and Highgate to the extreme north, were on the Quebec border.[4] The same year, New Hampshire settlers moved onto land just north of Massachusetts, very close to land clearly within the colony of New York.[5]

As the New Hampshire settlers put down roots, New York's designs continued. Tensions and land disputes mounted, and New York developed a firm claim on the Champlain Valley. Philip Skene, one of the English officers who helped expel the French, set up his own little fiefdom on the southernmost section of Lake Champlain. He had nearly eighty families working on his land. The men and women were employed in numerous economic endeavors. Within the fledgling community of Skenesborough, lumber and gristmills, a store, stables, barns and living quarters all went up. The residents built bridges, docks and wharves. Slavery was still practiced in the northern colonies, and Skene and the families on his land had as many as thirty-seven slaves.[6]

Another New York settlement was set up in the western areas of Lake Champlain. In 1765, William Gilliland purchased land about twenty miles north of Crown Point. His effort was not as large as Skene's, but it featured a water-powered sawmill, perhaps the most important venture at the time.

To the north, land ownership and economic interests were still being worked out. The village of St. Jean rested on the Richelieu River, the approximate halfway point between Lake Champlain and the markets of Montreal. In 1765, the first land in what is today northern Vermont was carved up. In present-day Swanton, James Robertson, a trader from St. Jean, purchased land from the Abenaki. At least fourteen Abenaki families still lived on the banks of the Missisquoi River.[7] They witnessed most of the French settlers depart and encountered the first English Americans grabbing territory. Headquartered in St. Jean, Robertson likely restarted the lumbering operation on the banks of the Missisquoi River that had been destroyed during the French and Indian War.[8] The new sawmill was apparently in operation as early as September 1766.[9]

Economic interests in the area started to take off. In 1767, another sawmill was established on the Saranac River, near present-day Plattsburgh.[10] Just two years later, two more sawmills went up, this time on the eastern shores of the lake. One was on Otter Creek. Another was near present-day Shelburne, taking advantage of access to Quebec markets.[11]

In the fall and winter of 1767, Ethan Allen made his first journeys into the Green Mountains. He embarked on long hunting expeditions that took him away from his family in Connecticut and allowed him to sell furs to isolated New England markets.[12] It was during these first expeditions that Allen encountered the players involved in the property issues between the colonies.

Within the rest of the thirteen colonies, attitudes about England changed. During the French and Indian War, France was England's mortal enemy, and redcoats and militiamen were united in expelling that enemy from North America. After the war, the Crown used taxation and trade policy to raise money. Entire armies of English soldiers had fought and died defending North America. Why, the monarchy wondered, shouldn't the colonists help pay for the protection they received? New England bore the brunt of the new policies and was largely responsible for confrontations with English tax collectors and troops.

Over the next ten years, people began to look differently at the mother country. England was an ocean away. The colonies had developed small-

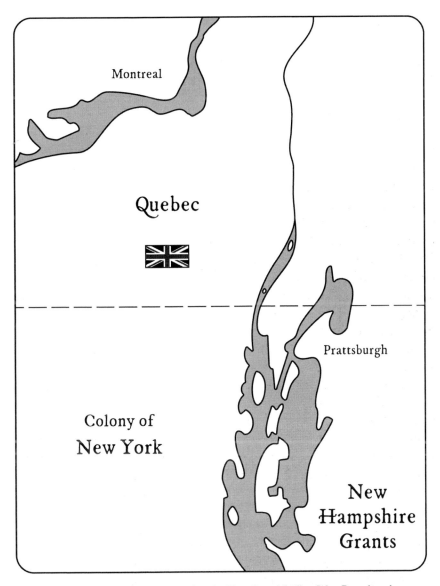

When New York colonists moved in after the French and Indian War, Prattsburgh was one of the frontier settlements. *Artwork by Lindsay DiDio.*

town participatory government, but the monarchy believed its colonies existed for the support and benefit of the homeland. As time passed, more colonists questioned whether they needed to maintain their allegiance.

England underestimated the frustration of its North American subjects. Someone born in Massachusetts in 1680 or in Connecticut in 1720 had

The location where Lake Champlain empties into the Richelieu River. This was the main transportation route to Montreal. *Photo by Armand Messier and Northern Vermont Aerial Photography.*

never been to England. They were raised as English subjects but had no real-world association with that nation or government. From their perspective, bloody wars might not even be necessary, if one greedy monarch simply left another greedy monarch alone.

When England, perhaps rightly, tried to raise money through tax and trade policies, there was an immediate backlash. In 1764, England enacted the Sugar Act. The colonies weren't allowed to acquire sugar or molasses from France, Spain or the Dutch. Trade officials and courts applied stiff penalties to those trying to work around the new policies. "No taxation without representation" became the cry of many. The Currency Act only caused more problems. It mandated that the colonies use England's money system, rather than the small currencies that had been developing locally. Most colonists didn't have access to gold or silver, and this further stressed the small but growing economies. The rarely used Quartering Act followed. It decreed that the colonists house British soldiers in their homes. There was further uproar with the Stamp Act of 1765, which put a tax on all paper use and required all sheets be marked with a revenue stamp. Lawyers and publishers, rather influential in the populated areas, publicly turned against the Crown.

Tensions further escalated with the Townshend Acts, which placed taxes on paper, paints, glass and tea. England was determined to see its new policies through. When protests took place in New England, British soldiers were sent to Boston to make sure the population knew who was in charge.

The shores of Lake Champlain, far from public-policy disputes and the growing tensions, became an inviting place to do business. England was certainly in charge, but the Champlain Valley was the frontier.

Meanwhile, the disputes between New Hampshire and New York continued. The tensions were geographic in nature, but opposing settlers came face to face in isolated forests, in valleys and along the open waterways of the lake.

The greater tensions were a world away.

Locally, New York's Simon Metcalf surveyed the Missisquoi Bay area in 1768.[13] This work helped that colony establish county boundaries on the east side of Lake Champlain.

Chapter 2

"ON THE ROAD TO REVOLUTION"

1770 to Early 1775

Moving the British military to Boston did not have the desired effect of quelling protest and dissension.

Two thousand English soldiers were deployed to Boston in September 1768. The redcoats were not received with open arms; the more adversarial colonists saw them as an occupying army.

The situation quickly deteriorated in February 1770. In one incident, a customs officer discharged his weapon while defending a Loyalist store against a mob of revolutionaries. An eleven-year-old child was killed. Weeks later, mobs of colonials openly harassed British soldiers on the streets. Threats were made. Snowballs and rocks were thrown. A British soldier discharged his rifle, probably in self-defense, and in the chaos, several other soldiers fired. Six Americans were wounded and five were killed. One of the five was Crispus Attucks, an African American. With shots fired and Americans killed in Boston, a broader, larger conflict seemed inevitable.

Around May 6, 1771, Simon Metcalf and his son completed a survey of the land east of Missisquoi Bay within New York's Albany County.[14]

While the territorial standoff between New York and New Hampshire played out in the southern regions of the Green Mountains, this was not the case to the north. New York, with Skenesborough and a few other settlements well established on the southern tip of Champlain, was well ahead of New Hampshire in settling the area and staking a claim. While Benning Wentworth chartered towns that almost no one would see for years, New York had mapped out the area, established county boundaries and started to

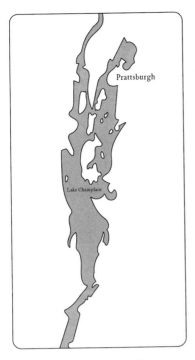

Prattsburgh became a small hub of economic activity in the early 1770s. *Artwork by Lindsay DiDio.*

develop its economic future. Many of the trade goods that arrived in the Champlain Valley originated in markets in Montreal and Quebec City. All of the timber harvested from the lake flowed north.

In July 1771, Metcalf, who was associated with New York, took over the small settlement James Robertson had restarted on the banks of the Missisquoi River in present-day Swanton. In New York court documents, his settlement was simply identified as the "Metcalf Tract."[15]

Within this land, which likely hosted a few French Canadian settlers and Abenaki tribesmen, was the village of Taquahunga Falls. Metcalf, a businessman, maintained his relationship with James Robertson, who may have moved north to St. Jean, Quebec. It would take time for the new owner's vision and business sense to develop, but the area was a prime economic venture, so close to Canada.

The New York land charter for the area detailed the first non-Abenaki or non-French-speaking settlers. When New York land lawyers created Prattsburgh (again, different from Plattsburgh on the other side of Lake Champlain), Simon Metcalf's son George was only seven years old. His wife, Catherine, was included on the document. Other grantees were specified, but it is unclear if they ended up in the Missisquoi area. John Norman and Daniel Tayler were mentioned as corporals in the English military and are examples of soldiers being rewarded with tracts of land. Other fighting men listed in the New York grant were Alexander McKenzie, John Robertson, John Fotheringham, John Kerns and William Crawford.[16]

When Metcalf set up shop, he created a small but crucial hub of activity that was important for years to come. Fine timber was ripe for harvest along the winding path of the Missisquoi River. A second benefit was the fur trade, with the valuable pelts of beaver and muskrat harvested in the swamps and marshes. The location wasn't perfect, as the Missisquoi River emptied into the isolated waters of Missisquoi Bay. Trading relied on access to open

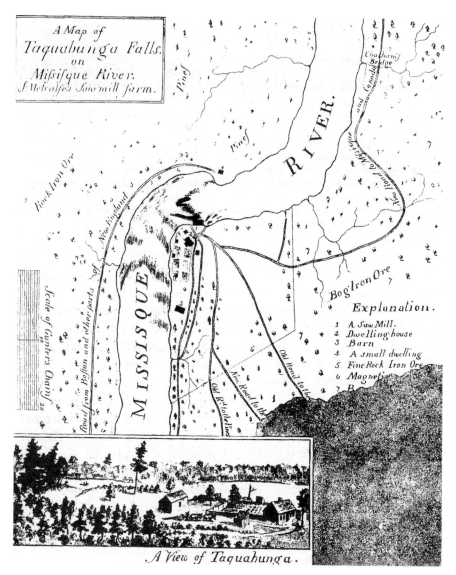

The layout of Simon Metcalf's settlement was captured on one of his maps. *Courtesy of the Swanton Historical Society.*

water. The town of Alburgh is a peninsula that juts into the broader lake. The islands of North Hero and Isle La Motte also obstructed travel. Boats moving in or out of Missisquoi Bay needed to navigate elaborate S curves to get to the Richelieu River and reach Canadian markets. Also, the Missisquoi River delta, shaped like the webbing of a duck's foot, faces almost due north

Metcalf's farm and sawmill employed Frenchmen from the first Quebec settlement and some Missisquoi Abenaki. *Artwork by Ashley Bowen.*

inside of the bay. It was a prime area to develop, but the transportation of goods wasn't easy.

Metcalf set up a trading post at the tip of the delta, a central location that allowed him to do business with everyone living in or visiting the area.[17] The land is still known today as Metcalf's Island. The Missisquoi Abenaki visited and did business at the post. Other Abenaki bands from the north visited. Local French merchants and farmers used it as a stopover point.

Metcalf took possession of the land, which at this early point was uncommon for the time with many New York land claims. New York created a county structure, which established large boundaries. But its effort to map out actual townships lagged well behind New Hampshire. New York settlements took hold and prospered in the Connecticut River valley, but their claims in the Champlain Valley were known as "paper towns." They may have existed on certain maps, but settlers from the New Hampshire Grants were in competition for the land. It appears as though Metcalf's land was far enough away from the disputes that he remained unmolested by the Green Mountain Boys.

At the time that Metcalf's settlement started to prosper, the English government attempted to mark where the frontier borders were. Putting a line on a map was easy enough, but finding those real locations in forests and measuring distances was a different matter. On the west side of Champlain, the perceived boundary between New York and Quebec was the forty-fifth parallel. The same applied on the Vermont-Quebec border. Much of this work was not done until 1771 and 1772.[18] It was undertaken by a pair of mapmakers and surveyors; Thomas Valentine and John Collins. Metcalf appears to have helped identify the Quebec boundary with New York under the leadership of New York's Alexander Colden in 1771.[19] Officials in New York and Quebec were interested in having the boundary laid out to the east. Those plans were developed in March 1772. Dealing with the late winter was problematic, as the ice was not very thick on parts of the lake. As Collins's party traveled north, a few of his horses broke through the ice. The travelers were not able to save the animals.[20] The boundary was imprecise, and the goal was to create a firm, visible border between Quebec and New England. They used Simon Metcalf's border calculations and Collins's own measurements.[21] New York's governor William Tryon called for the borderline to be established on the eastern side of the Richelieu River, all the way across the Green Mountains to the Connecticut River. The work involved creating piles of rocks every three miles and clearing and notching trees. Those trees in direct line of sight from one compass marker to the next were cut down.

Valentine and Collins met in Quebec, just north of New York State, at the mouth of the Lacolle River.[22] Approximately twenty workers started out just north of Windmill Point. The first part of their work probably went quickly; Alburgh is only about five miles wide. As they marked and cut trees and then piled rocks to mark the boundary, they emerged west of Missisquoi Bay. With the ice in such a fragile state, they carefully moved their equipment across the bay and commenced wood cutting in present-day Highgate, Vermont, and Philipsburg, Quebec. Spring rains slowed the project considerably. It is not known how much contact the team had with Simon Metcalf's settlement. However, just a few miles separated the isolated outpost and the survey crews. After the wet season, work resumed in June. Valentine noted in a letter that the work crews used the Missisquoi River to reach isolated areas to the east.[23] By September 1772, they had reached the Connecticut River. They had measured and marked ninety and one-quarter miles. The Abenaki were quite displeased at different points along the way, as their traditional hunting grounds had been disturbed.

For those coming from more populated regions, the settlement at Missisquoi was a light in the darkness. The closest settlements were quite distant. To the north was St. Jean, nearly a full day away. To the south, the Onion River was just barely being settled. Remember Baker, family relation to the Allens; Ira Allen; and another associate drove off a group of Yorkers, then surveyed the land. Allen threatened to kill them if they came back to the river.[24] Ironically, the Allen survey had departed from land owned by Philip Skene.[25] The relationship between Skene and the Allens has garnered the interest of modern scholars. The Allens built a military-style blockhouse

New York surveyors employed workers from Quebec to chop down trees along Missisquoi Bay for the border. *Artwork by Josh Sinz*.

on the Onion River as a signal to New Yorkers to stay away. They also discovered a group of New Yorkers already settled in present-day Shelburne. This group agreed to avoid trouble and purchase the land through New Hampshire's claim. These events were escalations between the "Bennington Mob," as the Allens were called, and settlers from New York. The Allens had

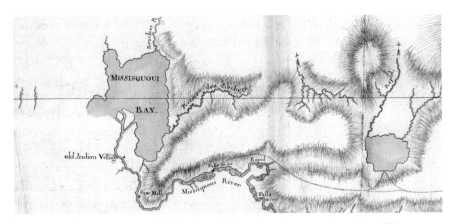

This early border map depicts the Missisquoi River along the recently cut forty-fifth parallel. *Courtesy of the Library of Congress.*

another blockhouse erected in the area of New Haven and Vergennes to halt repeated efforts by Yorkers to settle there.[26]

Isolated and far from other locations, Metcalf's settlement was the largest in the northern Green Mountains. Unfortunately for him, the reach of the Allen family would eventually extend into the northwest corner of the state.[27] Levi Allen, under the umbrella of the Onion River Land Company, made land purchases in Swanton.

Another New York settlement in the disputed territories was in Newbury, on the Connecticut River.[28] Jacob Bayley started the town. In the 1770s, he feared the influence of the Allens.

As time passed, Governor Tryon of New York wanted the boundary between New York and Quebec finalized and arranged for Collins and Valentine to resume their work. The laying of the border started up again in 1773.

More people moved into the region. Jesse Weldon and a few others put down roots in St. Albans Bay.[29] They were the first whites to build homes there.

Meanwhile, northern New York interested more colonials. One group of fifty families was associated with William Gilliland, who had started the sawmill on the Bouquet River years prior. Gilliland saw the economic potential of the Chazy River and requested regional protection by English forces.[30]

England's Quebec Acts brought the tensions between colonists and the mother country to a higher level. French Catholics north of the forty-fifth parallel were essentially left alone, which was not what the Protestants in the other colonies wanted. French civil law remained in Quebec, while British troops maintained order in parts of New England. The most offensive provisions of the acts were geographic.[31] The king cut off westward expansion in favor of Quebec's southern boundaries, upsetting colonists from New Hampshire to Georgia. The existing colonies were not going to be allowed to expand westward.

By 1774, the British military, the most efficient fighting force in the world, could no longer ignore the threat of armed conflict with its own subjects. Alongside attempts to quell dissent in Boston and punish Massachusetts, the Champlain Valley received notable military attention. First, British engineers assessed the condition and value of Crown Point and Ticonderoga. The Lake Champlain infrastructure, in northern Vermont's backyard, was significantly improved. The British military constructed a base at Point au Fer, New York, just northwest of Isle La Motte, due west of Alburgh and a few miles from Metcalf's settlement. The land juts out like an overhang at the top of a cliff. Sentries could keep an eye on north–south boat activity. It was a two-story structure, about fifty feet long and forty feet wide, and was constructed with stone walls nearly three feet thick. The cellar contained a well, a magazine containing weapons and supplies and forty cannon ports. On the second floor, a sentry box was located on each corner. The roof was double boarded and covered with shingles. It became known as the "White Building."[32] Some of William Gilliland's isolated settlers, located inland on the Great Chazy River, probably helped construct the building.[33] Anyone traveling south onto Lake Champlain

When tensions mounted between England and the colonies, the Point au Fer "White House" was erected to monitor northern Lake Champlain. *Artwork by Ashley Bowen.*

from the Richelieu River, perhaps trading with Metcalf in Missisquoi Bay, saw this tall, impressive building.

In Colchester, in June 1774, considerable work was done below the falls near the Fort Frederick Blockhouse on the Onion River. Remember Baker, Joseph Fuller, Henry Colvin and others cleared land for homesteads. They encountered an old Frenchmen named "Mallet" who lived somewhere in the vicinity of Mallet's Bay.[34]

At some point during the quiet summer or fall of 1774, English lieutenant John André, who would later play an intimate role in the fate of Benedict Arnold, sailed up the Hudson River valley and visited Fort Ticonderoga and Crown Point.[35] His path took him farther north on Lake Champlain, between the Point au Fer "White House" and Metcalf's settlement.

Prominent names looked to leapfrog the influence of both New Hampshire and New York colonial governments. Ethan Allen and Philip Skene recognized that the best solution for the Green Mountains was independence from the two feuding colonies. They initiated a push for autonomy from the two.[36] Skene departed for England with a proposal to create a separate colony bordering Quebec.

Finally, as a prelude to just how uniquely situated northwest Vermont was, the plotting colonies initiated spy missions against the Crown. At least one went through the northern edge of the Champlain Valley. The Massachusetts Committee of Correspondence wanted information about the size and strength of British forces in Quebec. If war came, the revolutionary schemers wanted quality intelligence. John Brown, a lawyer from Pittsfield, Massachusetts, was given the recon mission.[37] It occurred in very early 1775, and he went through the northern Green Mountains. A Native American, Winthrop Hoit, served as his guide and escort.[38] He arrived in Montreal and tried to assess if the French inhabitants would favor a revolt against the Crown.[39]

Tensions were high, but war had not broken out.

In central areas of the Green Mountains, a man named Roger Stevens bought and sold different tracts of property. He owned land on Otter Creek near Pittsford and had a hand in starting a gristmill and a sawmill. He had sympathies with the British government that played out in varying ways.[40] He was one of many.

Chapter 3

"MISSISQUOI ON THE MAP"

Spring and Fall of 1775

S ettlers, hoping that everything would remain peaceful, went about their lives. In present-day Williston, two men, Amos Robinson and John Chamberlain, established homesteads.[41] They put down roots in the ideal countryside of the Green Mountains. By 1775, another blockhouse had been built. This time, it was erected by the Pierson family on land in the town of Shelburne.[42]

Outside of the Champlain Valley, British commanders believed it was time to quash activity that might lead to armed rebellion. On a tense morning in late April outside Boston, they sent troops to the towns of Lexington and Concord, where revolutionaries had stored weapons. The soldiers arrived at Lexington, and the local militia stood its ground. The "shot heard 'round the world" rang out, and small, isolated events cascaded out of control. It was like a single rock rolling down the edge of a mountain, turning into an avalanche. The British suffered heavy casualities as marksmen picked them off from behind stone fences and trees. The minutemen soldiers handled themselves well against trained, professional troops. Blood had been spilled, and an anxious New England countryside waited for what might happen next.

Not all colonials agreed on the next course of action. In New Haven, Connecticut, Benedict Arnold and a man named David Wooster engaged in a stare down over the community's weapons and supplies. Arnold, who would become the most important figure in Champlain Valley's Revolutionary War history, wanted the weapons rushed east toward Boston.[43] As colonial militias gathered around the city, rebel leaders plotted how they could stand up to the British army on the battlefield. The Americans required cannons; none were available in the Boston area.[44]

The Champlain Valley was a different matter, however.

Benedict Arnold and others knew of the lightly guarded British garrisons on Lake Champlain. Their cannons were essential for any long-term conflict. Conversations were held, plots hatched and missions undertaken that made the Champlain Valley the critical theater of the developing conflict. Arnold, who participated in some of the conversations that led to the plans against Ticonderoga and Crown Point, received a colonel's

Benedict Arnold led the early Revolutionary War effort in the Champlain Valley. *Courtesy of the Library of Congress.*

commission from Massachusetts. Others initiated plans to attack the British forts, too. Some knew of the aggressiveness of Ethan Allen and the Green Mountain Boys and enlisted them in the plot. Secrecy was of the utmost importance. The forts and the valuable cannons in them needed to be taken before news of hostilities reached the area. In early May, the Green Mountain Boys assembled and moved north from Bennington. Arnold, who was still gathering supplies and volunteers in southern New England, heard that the plot was already underway. He dispatched advisors to recruit and gather men. Arnold departed for the Green Mountains, determined to lead the venture.

On May 8, he caught up with the Green Mountain Boys. Prizing their frontier independence, Allen's men wanted to lead the charge, but hotheaded Arnold attempted to take control. Eventually, a joint command was agreed to. Fort Ticonderoga was not the only objective. Nearby Skenesborough was a Loyalist settlement, and a small group under the command of Captain Herrick was dispatched to neutralize them. Another goal was to capture Philip Skene's personal sailing vessel, the schooner *Katherine*.[45] Word was also sent north to the Onion River, where Remember Baker and others had settled. They were to grab their muskets and join yet another group moving against Crown Point.[46] Early on the morning of May 10, Allen, Arnold and eighty-three others took Fort Ticonderoga. The

Revolution was no longer an isolated conflict unfolding around Boston. In a matter of days, it had gotten much larger.

The difference between the rough-and-tumble Green Mountain backwoodsman, Allen, and the experienced seaman, Arnold, came to a head in the days after Ticonderoga fell. Many believed taking the forts and wresting control of the cannons would be victory enough. Arnold understood that control of the land meant nothing without ships that controlled the waterways. After three or four days of watching Allen's men pillage and party, Arnold's men arrived from Connecticut and Massachusetts. He sent for the *Katherine*, renamed it *Liberty* and armed it with a few swivel and carriage guns. His attention turned to the northern end of Lake Champlain.[47]

As the *Liberty* moved north on the open waters, it encountered a smaller boat moving south. Arnold's men boarded and discovered it was the mail courier from St. Jean to Fort Ticonderoga. Arnold's aggressiveness handed the American cause a treasure trove of information. Among the mail seized was correspondence between British generals Guy Carleton and Gage in Boston. The documents provided the official count of the British army in Quebec. There were less than eight hundred British soldiers serving on Lake Champlain and in Quebec.

Poor winds on the night of May 16 prevented *Liberty* from moving any farther north than Point au Fer, in present-day Champlain, New York.[48] Arnold, with thirty-five men in two bateaux, rowed all night and arrived at

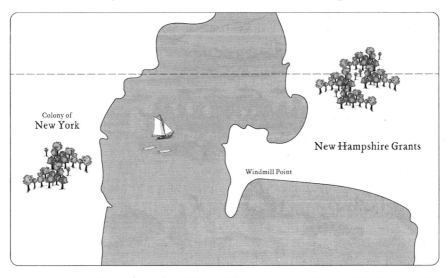

Arnold sailed the *Liberty* by Alburgh's Windmill Point in May 1775. *Artwork by Lindsay DiDio.*

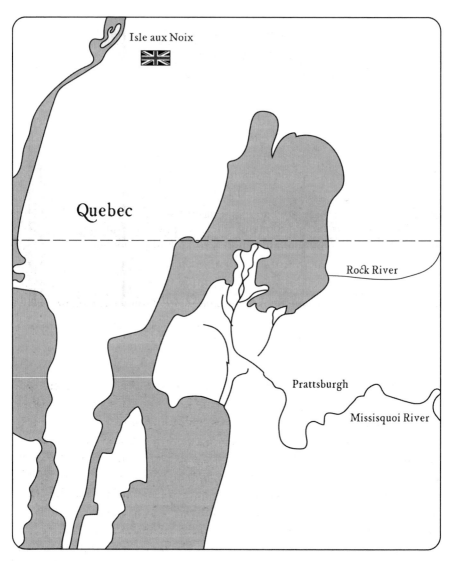

Arnold's raid into Quebec unfolded in northern Vermont's backyard. *Artwork by Lindsay DiDio.*

St. Jean at 6:00 a.m. on May 17. The raid's objective was to seize that which might give the British a chance to take back control of Lake Champlain. Arnold captured the sloop docked at St. Jean. Some historical sources have this vessel dubbed the *Betsy*; others have it named the *George*.

It was now the second vessel of the American navy, and Arnold renamed it *Enterprise*.[49] During the brief occupation, a local man by the name of Moses

Benedict Arnold and Ethan Allen led separate raiding parties north of Alburgh. *Photo by Armand Messier and Northern Vermont Aerial Photography.*

Hazen approached Arnold about the rebel activity. Hazen was a complex figure who came to support the rebel cause, and his military career would have a lasting impact in the northern Green Mountains.

Arnold was aware of British reinforcements moving down from Chambly and Montreal that could arrive at any moment. With control of the sloop and the schooner, the British were not an immediate threat on Lake Champlain. The rebels departed for safety and encountered Ethan Allen and the Green Mountain Boys packed into four bateaux. They were exhausted, tired and hungry but determined to pull off something Arnold had decided against: attacking and holding Fort St. Jean.[50] Arnold shared what supplies he had and attempted to dissuade them, but they did not listen. The *Enterprise* and *Liberty* continued south while Allen rowed north. The attempt was short-lived. After camping on the banks of the Richelieu River for one night and waking up to cannon fire, the Green Mountain Boys retreated back down the Richelieu, past Windmill Point.

Events soon took on a life of their own. With the two vessels docked at Ticonderoga, colonials received intelligence that the British had bolstered their presence at St. Jean and were engaged in preparations to take back the lake. The news was not unexpected. *Enterprise* and *Liberty* were further armed and upgraded. To strengthen the colonial position around Boston, cannons were removed from Fort Ticonderoga and Crown Point and prepared for transport to southern New England. Phillip Skene's slaves were conscripted to help with this effort.[51] Arnold's boldness in capturing two sailing vessels influenced some New York landowners in the area. William Gilliland, with his large tracts of land and growing settlements, wrote the Continental Congress as early as May 29. He urged an invasion of Quebec and proposed that the Point au Fer White House be upgraded, manned by revolutionaries and used to support soldiers moving north.[52]

While the rebels had seized Lake Champlain, the British forces in Quebec were in a decent position. They still controlled all of Quebec, were the most accomplished sailors in the world and could threaten Lake Champlain if left alone. The tiny Richelieu River was to play a key role in any future military operations.

Near the mouth of the Richelieu, northwest of Missisquoi Bay and due north of the town of Alburgh, Vermont, is the strategically important tiny island of Île aux Noix. After the attacks of May, the British recognized its importance and sent survey teams to assess making the location more defendable. However, the emphasis quickly became defending St. Jean.[53]

Events developed sooner than the colonials wanted.

On June 4, after asking for volunteers to scout north, Arnold filled the *Liberty*, *Enterprise* and three armed bateaux with 155 men.[54] He was determined to prevent the British from descending onto Crown Point and Fort Ticonderoga. By June 6, the squadron had rowed and sailed beyond Point au Fer, trying to reach the narrows of the Richelieu.

They moved north of the forty-fifth parallel, toward Hospital Point, a mile or so north of Alburgh. Arnold sent scouting missions and learned the British were indeed fortifying St. Jean. The Americans moved farther north and occupied Île aux Noix, and a protracted skirmish unfolded. Arnold's force was little match against the three hundred British regulars. Squads of Americans approached St. Jean from the woods and sniped at British bateaux on the Richelieu. As late as June 8, Arnold still planned an assault against the defenders, wondering if he could bring the cannons of *Liberty* and *Enterprise* to his advantage. He decided that if the British were fortifying St. Jean, they were probably not an immediate threat to the southern areas of the lake. On the morning of June 9, his flotilla departed the Richelieu and sailed past Alburgh and Isle La Motte. By June 10, it was back at Crown Point.

During the final weeks of June, Ticonderoga, Crown Point and the northern theater underwent significant changes. Arnold's early efforts on

Champlain were squandered. As the colonial army took shape, there was little room for an aggressive, confrontational officer with a commission from Massachusetts alone. Other high-ranking officers showed up at Ticonderoga with commissions from the newly minted command structure specifically to supplant Arnold.

On June 19, Philip Schuyler was appointed one of three major generals in the new colonial army and assigned command of the Champlain Valley. While he was competent and qualified, politics influenced his ascent. He was a New Yorker and owned significant properties in the Hudson River valley. If the dispute with New Hampshire over the Green Mountains was going to be an issue, having a prominent New Yorker in charge was a nod to that colony's influence. That day, Arnold, who got along well with Schuyler, learned that his wife had passed away in Connecticut. He returned to New Haven to take care of his family affairs, turning his back on command issues that had arisen at Fort Ticonderoga.

One of the more unique journeys on the lake was that of Brooks Watson in late June. The Continental Congress provided a pass for Watson to escort a small group back home to Quebec. Riding in a bateau, Ira Allen and a squad of Green Mountain Boys escorted Watson's party north. Close to the forty-fifth parallel, west of the Champlain islands, the escorting party prepared for a possible ambush by enemy soldiers. Watson vehemently protested. Guns were drawn anyway, with young Ira Allen suspecting that Congress had been duped. The party was left on shore near the border, about three miles away from the nearest house. The escorts returned south, concerned they had just transported a Loyalist.[55] These suspicions were later confirmed.

Events outside the Champlain Valley spiraled out of control. The Battle of Bunker Hill took place near Boston, and news arrived at Ticonderoga days later. The colonials had inflicted heavy casualties but had been driven from their defensive positions. The reality of a longer war was setting in.

Colonial leaders agreed that an attempt to evict the British from Quebec was necessary. Plans were developed for an entire colonial invasion force to travel north, through northern Vermont's backyard. The bulk of this force organized at Crown Point and Fort Ticonderoga and consisted of the First, Second, Third and Fourth New York Regiments under the command of General Richard Montgomery.[56]

As the Americans organized, the enemy sent more reinforcements to St. Jean. Elements of the British Seventh Regiment, including the young Lieutenant John André, arrived during the summer.[57] British general Guy

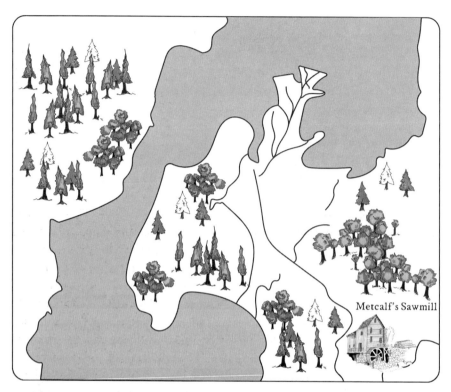

As Americans prepared for the invasion of Quebec, Metcalf's settlement in present-day Swanton provided critical information. *Artwork by Lindsay DiDio.*

Carleton believed that if the enemy could be stopped there, Quebec's winter would freeze the American offensive until spring. Reinforcements from England would arrive with the warmer weather.

By the middle of July, American vessels once again patrolled the northern edge of the lake. Remember Baker was on the *Liberty* on July 13. He operated near Missisquoi Bay and communicated with Simon Metcalf, a Mr. Sear and several Abenaki, seeking intelligence. Baker learned the enemy was more interested in taking prisoners than direct confrontation and that the British were busy improving the defenses of St. Jean. On July 16, Metcalf sent two individuals and a Native American child to the northwest, toward Île aux Noix and St. Jean. The *Liberty*, which had moved near Isle La Motte, encountered two canoes. The occupants provided what information they could.[58] Days went by. Metcalf and Sears were informed by local Frenchmen that their people had been taken in for questioning. Metcalf relayed information about the number of cannons at St. Jean and that there were nearly four hundred British regulars there. Baker persisted and scouted on his own. Near the forty-fifth parallel, he encountered more natives with contacts across the border. The news was favorable; tribes to the north had little interest in taking up arms against the Yankees. Baker's scouting mission ended, and he returned to Ticonderoga by July 26.[59] American command learned that English scouts also probed south, on the western shore of the lake.

The British still exerted influence over the region, and Simon Metcalf received word from Guy Carleton that he was permitted to remain on his property during this time of conflict.[60]

Another rebel scouting mission quickly took shape. Bayze Wells, who had just arrived in the region, was given the task of attaining more information about St. Jean. He left for Crown Point from Ticonderoga in a bateau on July 23. The next day, he joined with four other scouts, one of whom was John Brown, who'd reconned the area prior to the outbreak of hostilities. The journey north involved a short trip in a bateau and a quick rendezvous with the *Enterprise*, which had been operating south of Split Rock. All four men were transferred to the *Liberty* a bit farther north. Finally, they rowed again in their bateau. By the twenty-sixth, they had put in north of Cumberland Head and quietly navigated the dense forest. They maneuvered through the countryside, avoiding most Native Americans and locals. Enduring hard rain, on July 30 they reached the road between Montreal and St. Jean. August 1 was a tough day. After spending the night at a French *habitant*'s house near Chambly, they departed the next morning. Hours later, about fifty British regulars surrounded the house, now aware of the American mission. The pursuit began, and the Americans avoided patrols by moving east. Along the way, they caught a glimpse of St. Jean, where new British sailing ships were under construction.[61] They fled south, and the five men separated into two groups. On August 5, Wells and his partner spied Lake Champlain and crossed a creek with some difficulty. The location was likely Rock River in northern Highgate. The pair traveled for another three miles, came to the Missisquoi River and followed it to Metcalf's settlement. The other group of American spies had arrived shortly before them. Metcalf provided the men with a canoe so they could return to Fort Ti, traveling down the Missisquoi River and hugging the lakeshore near the present-day towns of Swanton, St. Albans, and Georgia. They rowed all night, traveling about thirty miles.[62] Eventually, they returned to the American bases.

While this mission wrapped up, the *Liberty* was still in the western branch of the lake, near Isle La Motte. On August 3, it anchored at the south end

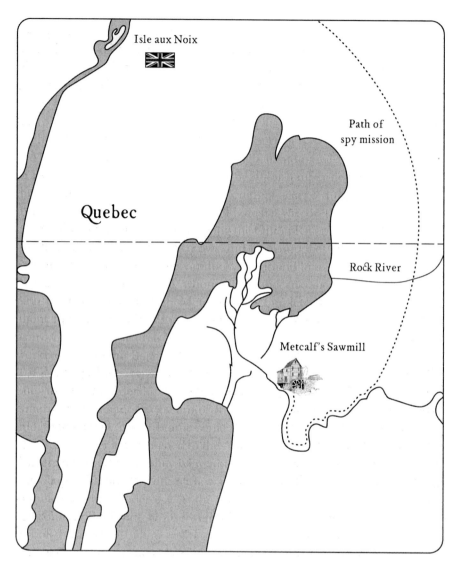

When Bayze Wells returned from his spy mission, he came through the woods of Highgate and Swanton. He waded through Rock River to get to the Missisquoi. *Artwork by Lindsay DiDio.*

of the island and a small force trekked north to check in with two different Frenchmen living there. They met up with Remember Baker, once again deployed to the region, now the eyes and ears of the army. One of the Frenchmen, Mr. Vandelowe, said some *habitants* were being held by the British and shared information about two large ships under construction at St. Jean.[63]

In early August, the Americans encountered an Englishman from Quebec with a pass to go to Missisquoi.[64] Mr. Duguid claimed to have left St. Jean twelve days earlier and desired to go to Gilliland's New York property. His purpose was to contact his wife's family, who lived on Gilliland's estate. He provided updated information on the defenses at Chambly and St. Jean. Perhaps the most valuable information was about stockpiled timber and English work crews constructing more vessels. The evidence was clear. The British were working to challenge the American presence below the forty-fifth parallel. Another traveler revealed that some native bands had joined the British at St. Jean and suggested that the Missisquoi Abenaki may have been among them.[65] That day, the *Enterprise* received its new captain, James Smith, who took command and expressed concern about its condition.[66]

American forces were slowly gathering, and the potential invasion of Quebec was getting closer. On August 6, General Schuyler wrote to George Washington about the need for the first companies of Timothy Bidel's unit to arrive in the Champlain Valley. Schuyler communicated his nervousness about local tribes, including the Missisquoi Abenaki, that might oppose the American invasion.[67]

Another scouting mission was undertaken by Bayze Wells on August 11. With Metcalf's canoe in tow, he and eleven others paddled up the lake's western shores. After two days, they retrieved their boat from the previous mission, just north of Cumberland Head. The men rowed east, S curving through the Champlain islands, and saw the house of a Frenchman, Mr. Tommo, likely on present-day North Hero. Just after sunrise on August 14, the men moved north, into Missisquoi Bay, keeping a cautious eye toward Quebec. They reached Metcalf's Island at the mouth of the Missisquoi and briefly separated. Six men brought their bateaux and the canoe into the river's narrow confines. They were at Metcalf's settlement for several hours. The other group waiting in the bay looked north-northwest, studied the Quebec shore and wondered if enemy soldiers were in the distant tree line. At three o'clock in the afternoon, Bayze Wells and his men returned, and the scouts began the long journey home.[68]

The need for information became even more critical. Another mission was underway west of Alburgh. The *Liberty*, operating near the New York shore, brought John Brown, Remember Baker and Captain Stewart to gather even more intelligence. They dropped off a man named Peter Griffin and a young native boy at about the same time that Bayze Wells was in Missisquoi Bay.[69] The child's father stayed on the *Liberty*. While Griffin and the boy were in Quebec, they hugged the west side of the Richelieu. One

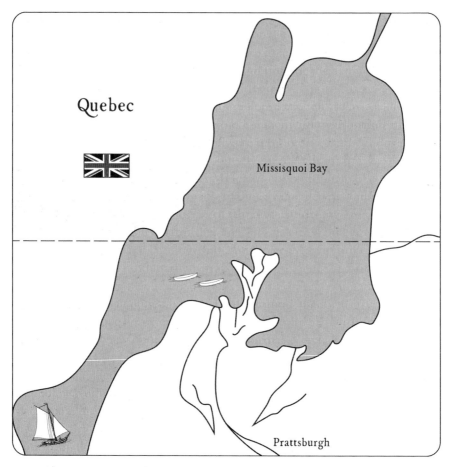

The location of Metcalf's settlement provided colonials with opportunities to gather information in Missisquoi Bay. *Artwork by Lindsay DiDio.*

night, they were at a sympathetic Frenchman's house, a Mr. Vinelagh's, just above the New York border. On August 22, nervous Griffin had been gone too long, and Captain Stewart sailed *Liberty* north of Windmill Point. He sounded the depths of the narrow river, aware that American vessels would pass through soon.[70] Sounding allowed him to know where larger vessels could navigate without their hulls scraping the river bottom. Additionally, the enemy might be distracted by the *Liberty* instead of looking for Griffin. He and the boy returned, and the report was rushed off to the American generals. They had observed further enemy activity at St. Jean.[71] The two new British vessels were nearing completion.

Remember Baker aggressively scouted north of Alburgh. He hid his boat along the shore. *Artwork by Josh Sinz.*

Being aggressive, Remember Baker wanted more information and set out with a few Green Mountain Boys toward Île aux Noix. The father and son whom he had just employed warned them about native patrols near St. Jean. Baker eluded the enemy and continued his information gathering.

It was a critical mistake.

Later that day, he was on the eastern side of the Richelieu, about five miles north of Alburgh and three miles from Île aux Noix. A small group of natives and a French Canadian, agents of the Crown, discovered Baker's boat and attempted to confiscate it. The squad of Green Mountain Boys tried to stop them, an altercation ensued and shots were fired.[72] Remember Baker was killed, shot through head. Some of the natives were injured.[73] They cut off his head and brought it to the English soldiers at St. Jean.[74] He was the first casualty of the American invasion of Quebec. The British army spread propaganda among the natives and *habitants*, claiming Baker was ordered to treat them harshly prior to the invasion.[75]

When the American leadership found out about the incident, they were understandably nervous. The route into Quebec traversed the ancestral homeland of native groups allied with the British. An opportunity to drive a wedge between those allies had been lost, and because of Remember Baker, the Americans might not be seen as liberators. The American flotilla was days away from beginning the invasion. General Schuyler attempted to send overtures to the Six Nations of the Iroquois and other bands before events escalated further. He kept George Washington apprised of the situation.[76]

On August 28, barely three months after Ethan Allen and Benedict Arnold had wrested area forts from the British, rebel forces launched the Quebec invasion. Nearly 1,200 colonial soldiers departed Crown Point and Fort Ticonderoga and sailed north on Lake Champlain. Their first destination was Isle La Motte. The vanguard of the fleet arrived on August 31. Scouts immediately scoured northern regions of the island. The larger sailing vessels, the *Enterprise* and *Liberty*, were off the western shore of the island. Two new gunboats, the *Schuyler* and the *Hancock*, built during the summer, joined them. Scores of bateaux ferried more soldiers north.

On August 31, the weather changed, and the Champlain Valley was subject to windy and rainy weather.[77] That evening, and over the next few days, the entire American army gathered on the tiny Vermont island of Isle La Motte.[78] The foul weather prevented the soldiers from moving north. By September 4, the invasion recommenced. Hundreds of Americans streamed into the Richelieu River. Foreshadowing events to come, almost two hundred soldiers remained on the island, already ill. Scouts fanned out on the western shore of the Richelieu. Troops also moved along the eastern shore, directly north of Missisquoi Bay. The northern shoulder of the Green Mountains was now the flank of an entire American invasion force.

By September 6, most of the army was at Île aux Noix. Generals Schuyler and Montgomery launched their assault against St. Jean. It did not go well. First, Île aux Noix was approximately twelve miles south if its target. For the Americans to attack, they had to sail a straight section of the Richelieu. Any move against St. Jean would be seen and reported. Second, they were about to attack an easily defendable position. The outnumbered defenders were not going to surrender immediately. Finally, the Americans confirmed the reports from the summer: the British had nearly completed two large, fifty-two-foot-long sailing vessels. The Americans were stung when the first attack was repulsed, so they sent part of their force up the Richelieu River, toward Fort Chambly. As the colonials struggled to tighten their grip, Schuyler made defensive improvements to Île aux Noix. He ordered a series of chain barriers installed on both sides of the river to prevent British shipping from bypassing the tiny island. They also improved the trenching. Île aux Noix served as the American headquarters for the unfolding invasion of Quebec.[79]

On September 12, Schuyler's health worsened, and he gave command of the invasion to Richard Montgomery. The commanding general departed Île aux Noix in a covered bateau and returned south. On the way, he met Seth Warner and approximately 170 Green Mountain Boys arriving to

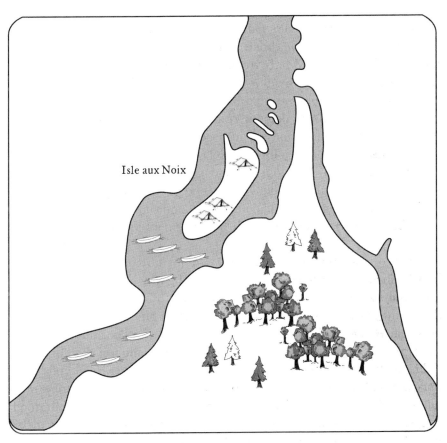

Isle aux Noix

The entire colonial army camped at Île aux Noix as it invaded Quebec. This is just a few short miles from Alburgh and Missisquoi Bay. *Artwork by Lindsay DiDio.*

support the invasion.[80] Among this group was Ebenezer Allen, a cousin of the Allen brothers. They entered Quebec at the head of the Richelieu.[81]

What unfolded around St. Jean was a classic siege. With each passing day, the American army tightened its grip, cutting off the small riverside town.

However, on September 25, Ethan Allen, whom many identify as a hero, took a course of action that removed him from participating further in the American Revolution. Allen believed he could take Montreal ahead of the rest of the army, with barely one hundred men. His force was immediately captured, denying Montgomery the extra help he needed. Allen spent the next eighteen months in prison.

The Americans had hoped the French *habitants* would support the invasion en masse. While some jumped at the chance to throw off the English, it was a fraction of what was hoped for. From the start, the invaders had unrealistic expectations. One local, who was apparently an Englishmen, did rise to the cause: Moses Hazen. Hazen's initial history with the American Revolution was already somewhat checkered. He was in a unique position, with businesses on the banks of the Richelieu just south and opposite the British garrison at St. Jean. He had provided intelligence for Benedict Arnold's raid in May, when the king's sloop was seized. At the time, unknown to the Americans, and perhaps hedging his bets, Hazen was the source that informed the British in Montreal of the American military activity. Now, with the entire American army surrounding his property and his assets being damaged by the exchanges of fire, Hazen threw in with the Americans. It was much easier to transact business with the army on his property than the one retreating north. His true loyalties were called into question, but the location of his property meant colonials had a dominating presence along the Richelieu.[82]

Down in Missisquoi Bay, Simon Metcalf was forced into making a similar decision. He was principally a businessman. Circumstances had put his sawmill, trading post and property on the back porch of the invasion. Metcalf started to sell goods directly to the American army.[83] Hazen's sawmill on the Richelieu was damaged in the siege of St. Jean, and Metcalf's was close enough for the colonials to take advantage of.

The Americans continued to squeeze the small town and fort at St. Jean. It had not been resupplied since the colonials crossed the border, and rations dwindled. The American situation wasn't great, either. Illness continued to be a huge issue. The weather was getting colder by the week. It had taken much longer than planned to bring up the appropriate cannons. Now into October, the British defenders still held out.

A critical event in the siege of St. Jean was the capture of Fort Chambly, just a few miles to the north. It fell to Montgomery's army on October 18. The supplies and cannons were quickly ushered south.

With the arrival of the colder weather, the Americans pushed reinforcements up the Lake Champlain corridor as fast as possible. General David Wooster, whom Benedict Arnold had clashed with immediately after Lexington and Concord, arrived at Fort Ticonderoga with a regiment of over three hundred men. Wooster's path, along with that of hundreds of others, took him along Vermont's Lake Champlain islands.[84]

With the colonial army now in Quebec, Lake Champlain turned into the continent's most important military transportation route. Well over one thousand soldiers had moved from Isle La Motte north. It took a lot of resources to feed an army, and every available bateau moved between the Richelieu River and Ticonderoga, keeping the army fed. Getting the food to them was very difficult. Each man was supposed to have an allotment of soap. The water sometimes wasn't the cleanest, so the army tried to furnish one quart of spruce beer per man each day. They were to get one-half pint of rice or one pint of Indian meal per week. If it was available, they got one pint of milk per day. Each man was supposed to get three pints of beans or peas, one pound of bread and about one pound of beef, pork or salt fish each day.[85] *Enterprise*, *Liberty* and all the bateaux were crammed with soldiers reinforcing the invasion. When available, the vessels were stuffed with barrels and crates of food.

With the noose closing around St. Jean, the British in Montreal attempted to lift the siege on October 30. Seth Warner and the Green Mountain Boys repulsed the attack. Carleton, who saw the writing on the wall, started to prepare for the evacuation of the city. Montreal, even with nearly one thousand defenders, would become an undefendable location. It rested on the St. Lawrence to the west of the Richelieu River. Carleton knew he stood a better chance of defending Quebec City, much farther to the east. St. Jean capitulated on November 2. The victorious Americans swept up to the St. Lawrence, almost capturing Carleton, but he escaped to fight another day. Montreal surrendered to the Americans on November 13.

The American resupply effort succumbed to the nasty fall weather of northern New England. The Quebec winter approached. During the last weeks of November and through cold spells in December, ice formed in the shallowest waters, making bateau travel hazardous. To deal with the falling temperatures and the accumulating snow, the army procured and built numerous sleighs, to be pulled by horses and oxen. Boat travel was about to become nonexistent. Such travel was impossible through the Green Mountains, so the traditional routes, over the ice when it was cold enough, were maintained.[86]

Meanwhile, the British had suffered major defeats but still had a substantial fighting force at Quebec City. Carleton had assembled almost all of his forces there; nearly 1,200 British and allied soldiers were inside the city walls

In late 1775, Jacob Bayley, in the area of the northern Connecticut River, wrote a letter to George Washington about ways to reinforce the armies in Quebec. Bayley suggested the construction of a military road stretching from the Connecticut River to Missisquoi Bay. He referenced the mapping work of Simon Metcalf. Washington understood the importance of keeping the army healthy and resupplied and forwarded the suggestion to John

Hancock.[87] In peacetime, the idea of a road connecting the east and west sides of the Green Mountains had not been feasible. In war, all possible routes were under consideration.

The American invasion of Quebec had been successful to this point. Benedict Arnold had completed his trek through Maine with several hundred colonial soldiers and was at the gates of Quebec City. It took longer than anyone wanted, but Montgomery had moved his army north on the Richelieu, seized Montreal and joined Arnold.

Even though it was undeveloped wilderness, northern Vermont had become the major supply route for the American army attempting to expel the British from the continent.

Chapter 4

"THE COLD PULSE OF WAR"

Winter of 1775 Through Spring of 1776

The effort to claim Quebec hinged on taking Quebec City. Generals Arnold and Montgomery had surrounded the city, but conquering it at the onset of winter was difficult. A large defensive wall protected the settlement and favored the defenders. The American generals wanted the right weather before they attacked. New reinforcements were arriving, but many soldiers from the fall campaign would be able to go home at the start of the New Year. Their enlistments were up. With desertions, illness and the enlistment issue, Montgomery's overall numbers didn't even match the force they were about to attack. They needed to take Quebec City, as it was the port the English navy would sail into when the ice melted in the spring.

After weeks of difficulty, the attempt to take the city materialized on New Year's Eve. Snow arrived, helping to mask the approach of the colonial army. The assault did not go well. Montgomery, the senior commander, was killed in the attempt. Colonial soldiers became confused in the snowstorm and couldn't reach the places they needed to be to support other units. Arnold took a bullet to the leg, and the attempt collapsed.

Suddenly, the Quebec invasion was coming apart at the seams. Based on the first attempt, the remaining military leadership determined that an assault against the city's walls would not work. A large enough force had to be gathered, probably in spring, to make a second attempt.

Foreshadowing the larger problems to come, the Americans were in dire need of supplies. On January 2, just hours after suffering the near fatal leg wound, Arnold considered the amount of food, ammunition and blankets his army had. There was enough food for a little more than a week.[88] While the situation was not quite critical, the winter snows and brutally cold temperatures were only going to make resupply worse. However, there were no other options, and American leadership began to plan how to improve the resupply infrastructure.

On January 10, General Schuyler wrote to the president of Congress and suggested that Missisquoi Bay could turn into a regular stopping-off point as troops moved north on their way to Quebec.[89] The commanding general acknowledged the importance of Metcalf's location and its value to the army.

As the cold of January gripped the countryside, the head count of the colonial forces in Quebec didn't take much ledger space. The New York regiments were still present, but nearly everything else was a hodgepodge of understrength units. Promised units gathered from within Quebec; Colonel James Livingston's First Canadian Regiment and Lieutenant Colonel Duggan's battalion of Canadian Rangers weren't completely assembled yet. Those units were significantly understrength. Companies from John Fellow's Massachusetts unit weren't fully present. Parts of Seth Warner's regiment were present, but recruitment was still underway. David Wooster's men had finally arrived in Montreal, but under his poor leadership they did more harm than good. In fact, these men distrusted Benedict Arnold and did not obey some of his orders.[90]

Due to the freezing conditions, the constant stream of supply ships and bateaux that had gone back and forth between Crown Point and St. Jean came to a stop. Small, undersized units made the trek north, but the journey was uninviting at best. They departed Crown Point and Ticonderoga, which were already on the edge of the frontier. The frozen surface of Lake Champlain became the new road north. Soldiers slipped and stumbled and marched through blowing snow. Bone-chilling windchills sucked heat from their bodies. Undersized companies marched to the solid ground of Grand Isle, North Hero, South Hero, Isle La Motte and Alburgh. They found temporary sanctuary at St. Jean and then in Montreal, but Arnold

MAJOR GENERAL PHILIP SCHUYLER.

Philip Schuyler led the American invasion effort. *Courtesy of the Library of Congress.*

needed many more men. By January 13, General Wooster had received enough reinforcements that he could spare some for Arnold at Quebec City. Approximately 120 soldiers departed Montreal for points farther east.[91] More were not far behind.

By January 26, another 140 men had braved the Champlain route, stopped at Montreal and set out to join Arnold's forces.[92] At this time, Schuyler was still exploring Missisquoi Bay's importance on the route north.[93]

George Washington wanted soldiers in Quebec as soon as they could be raised. On February 1, he called on individual colonies to provide more men. In a letter to Timothy Bidel of New Hampshire, who had already raised one regiment for the initial invasion, Washington urged more units be assembled and rushed to the Onion River. There, they would join other forces gathering on Lake Champlain.[94] Writing from Montreal and hoping for more men, General Wooster communicated with General Bayley about the route through the Green Mountains to Missisquoi Bay.[95] They made plans for the next fighting season and explored which routes would get men to Quebec the fastest.

The Connecticut River was identified as a possible north–south route. Colonial units throughout New England could take bateaux all the way up to northern New Hampshire. Transportation was in doubt beyond that location, however. Soldiers could portage over rough terrain to Lake Memphremagog in the northeastern portion of the New Hampshire Grants and then march to the St. Lawrence River. This was not at all desirable because of the distances and terrain involved.

Another option was building a road through the Green Mountains. The project would have started in Newbury and emerged somewhere along Lake Champlain or the Richelieu River. Acknowledging the importance General Washington put on the fastest transportation routes, scouting for the road was undertaken in the middle of winter.

In Newbury, Jacob Bayley was at first unsuccessful in getting anyone to take the mission. Eventually, he convinced his nephew Frye Bayley and a few others. The men were assured they would be well paid. A local hunter, Bill Heath, and Silas and Abiel Chamberlain were the other recruits. They

George Washington was in constant communication with his generals about the importance of Missisquoi Bay. *Courtesy of the Library of Congress.*

left Newbury on February 1. That night, they stayed at Frye Bayley's house in Peacham. On the second day, they moved westward, encountering very deep snow. Disagreements immediately broke out. Abiel Chamberlain questioned the overall effort, and Silas suggested they return to camp. The men carried plenty of supplies, roughly sixty pounds each, but the trek seemed too daunting to complete. After agreeing to continue, they moved through snows sometimes five feet deep. At the end of the second day, they had traveled about eight miles to Joe's Pond. The third day was difficult, with the group making only six miles. They lodged in Woodbury for the night. They next trudged over the spine of the Green Mountains in snowshoes, and as darkness fell on February 5, they camped near the Lamoille River. After almost a week, the four men arrived at Metcalf's log house in present-day Swanton.[96] They spent the night and departed early the next morning. Frye and his companions followed the frozen Missisquoi River onto the ice of Missisquoi Bay. The next day, they arrived at St. Jean. The exhausted scouts contacted General Wooster in Montreal and confirmed that the route was traversable. They rested until February 11, when they began the return journey. They were in St. Jean by nightfall. By the twelfth, they were back at Metcalf's. Six days later, they returned to Newbury. By February 26, General Bayley had written a letter to Washington and confirmed that a road through the northern Green Mountains was now a viable option.[97]

In warfare, information is critical. And in early 1776, as plans for the road developed, Loyalists informed the British leadership about the emerging route.[98]

The weather became impossibly cold. In one case, an already exhausted and sickly American sentry outside of Quebec City stood guard in the blowing and freezing winds for so long that his eyes literally froze shut.[99] Men marching over the Lake Champlain ice experienced the same frigid temperatures as Arnold's forces had.

Reinforcements continued arriving; another twenty-five men reached Quebec on February 4. A few days later, a handful of Pennsylvania companies completed the trek north. When they departed Crown Point and Ticonderoga, General Schuyler noted that many of the men didn't have mittens or appropriate footwear.[100] It was a brutal march toward the Lake Champlain islands. A blizzard bore down on the Northeast during the second week of February. The snowdrifts in Quebec were so high that, in some cases, snow reached second-story windows.[101]

The Continental Congress became concerned about the situation. Generals were in regular contact with delegates, keeping them apprised

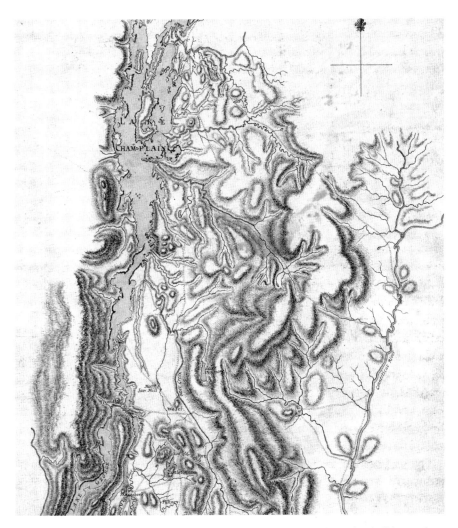

Simon Metcalf's early maps were used by the colonial army as it planned to build a road through the Green Mountains. *Courtesy of the Library of Congress.*

of the fall's successes and winter's failures. On February 17, the political leaders organized a commission to find out what was happening north of the forty-fifth parallel. The commission members were important players in the political machinations of the struggle for independence. Charles Carroll, Samuel Chase, John Carroll (who was a Catholic priest) and Benjamin Franklin were given the task.

In late February, more Massachusetts recruits arrived in Quebec. Companies in Captain Bellow's regiment marched through the snow and ice for days to get to the front lines. Sadly, some of them immediately succumbed to smallpox.[102]

As Arnold recovered from his leg wound, he tried to deal with the slow resupply and reinforcement effort. When he determined that the contents of some recently arrived sleighs were insufficient, he purchased twenty-seven cattle from locals in late February.[103] Schuyler, still commanding from southern regions of the Champlain Valley, also attempted to solve the supply situation. In a somewhat forward-thinking letter to Congress, he suggested cattle be raised in the area of the Onion River in Vermont.[104] If the army in Quebec could hold on and the supply infrastructure along Champlain developed, the land could be used to feed the northern armies.

On February 28, Wooster dispatched more reinforcements to Quebec City from Montreal.[105] Wooster's command style turned many local Catholics against the invaders. He had a few priests arrested and closed chapels.[106] These actions did nothing to persuade the French in Quebec to flock to the rebel cause. From tiny townships around Île aux Noix to the city of Montreal, local inhabitants had no interest in accepting American currency.[107]

By March 6, warmer weather had returned. It caused havoc with the fledgling resupply effort. The ice had partially broken up around Lake George, Crown Point and Fort Ticonderoga. While moving supplies north over Lake Champlain, a man and several horses drowned.[108] Despite these challenges, Arnold now had over 1,500 soldiers under his command.[109] By the end of March, that number had increased significantly, to over 2,500. Diseases began to spread, and almost one-third of Arnold's men had fallen ill.[110]

More reinforcements were on the way. In New Hampshire, Timothy Bidel's new regiment came together, but as of March 8, Captain Osgood's Company was still assembling.[111] Most of his men proceeded over the Green Mountains to the Onion River and joined the forces moving over Lake Champlain. Lagging, Osgood's detachment was ordered to proceed northwest over the Green Mountains, following the route established in early February. Frye Bayley was called on once again. They departed from Newbury on March 25 and set out for Metcalf's. Among the men in this unit were Lieutenant Sam Fowler, Second Lieutenant John Webster and Ensign Jeremiah Abbot.[112] Another, Captain Thomas Johnson, took notes for future use on the construction of the road. The company spent the night at Metcalf's on April 1.[113] That night, Metcalf and Johnson conversed about the routes through the mountains that might save the colonial army marching time. The company departed the next morning and was in Montreal by the seventh.

Osgood's Company marched through the Green Mountains and arrived at Simon Metcalf's settlement in March 1776. *Artwork by Ashley Bowen.*

As Osgood's Company traveled toward Prattsburgh, George Washington did not let the matter drop with colonial leadership. On March 26, he wrote to Samuel Adams, advising him to bring up the road's construction with Congress.[114]

In Quebec, Arnold was still trying to feed and clothe his men. Meager supplies arrived from Ticonderoga. On March 27, he bought more food from the locals, about 1,300 pounds of flour and fifteen bushels of peas.[115]

As March ended, General Schuyler wrote to George Washington, informing him that the northern end of Lake Champlain was almost free of ice.[116] With much of the ice out of the way, movement of supplies and reinforcements could resume by boat.

As the weather warmed, the American command still hoped fresh soldiers might be able to expel the British from Quebec. By the first week of April, Israel Maxwell's New Jersey Regiment had made its way north. Schuyler urged arriving command officers to not antagonize the population of Quebec.[117]

General Wooster, who spent the entire winter in the relative comforts of Montreal, finally proceeded east to evaluate the siege of Quebec City. He arrived on April 1, ninety days after the New Year's Eve assault had failed. While the weather warmed in the Northeast, colonial soldiers still moved supplies using sleighs to get through snow.[118]

The army command structure became involved as well. Major General John Thomas, who had successfully led the siege of Boston, was ordered to Quebec. At the time that Thomas made his Lake Champlain journey north, Schuyler was desperately building as many bateaux as possible to support the troop movements. He hoped to have seventy available as more units arrived.[119]

Captain Johnson, who had accompanied Osgood's Company from the Connecticut River to Metcalf's and then to Quebec, returned via the Richelieu River to Metcalf's settlement. Metcalf had followed through and provided detailed plans for the road through the Green Mountains.[120]

As the American army in Quebec grew, the diseases got worse, particularly smallpox. Sadly, the trees and flowers were not the only things budding in the first weeks of spring.

Smallpox was a devastating disease. It decimated the malnourished army that was already fighting in unsanitary conditions. Its progress through individuals and then groups strangled the American war effort. If a soldier was unknowingly infected, he actually felt fine for close to two weeks. Once

Metcalf provided specific plans for the military road through Vermont. *Artwork by Ashley Bowen.*

ill, symptoms like fever, aches, pains and sometimes vomiting took over. Doctors couldn't diagnose smallpox cases until after symptoms began. In the rugged Quebec countryside, the early symptoms were little different than what some soldiers experienced daily. If a skin rash appeared, it was the first indication the disease had taken hold. Soldiers often reported for duty after exposure, unknowingly spreading it. The rash usually started in the throat and mouth. It spread to the rest of the body, and the patient's skin swelled with multiple small bumps, which then filled with liquid. This stage would last four or five days. A high fever was very common, and the disease was most contagious at this point. The bumps turned to pustules all over the body. The slightest itching caused uncontrollable oozing. This lasted another few days and was the cause of many deaths.[121]

Some doctors went ahead with an inoculation procedure, a crude, early attempt at vaccinations. It involved taking tiny amounts of liquid from smallpox pustules and placing doses in cuts in the skin of uninfected soldiers. In some cases, it worked. Some men experienced only mild symptoms and then resumed their duties. Many others were not so fortunate and became extremely ill. Some command officers didn't want the inoculations to continue, as it taxed healthy soldiers with extra duties, particularly when so many were already sick.

The weather didn't help. It was still raw and cold, and as late as mid-April there was still some ice on Lake Champlain.[122] Early colonial excitement about a warm spring was dampened by a cool, unwelcoming April. Smallpox was so prevalent that General Wooster noted that soldiers coming to Quebec were likely to get sick.[123]

To add to the worsening situation, Arnold and Wooster couldn't get along. Wooster was the superior officer, and Arnold was asked to take command in Montreal.

Meanwhile, Jacob Bayley wanted Washington and Schuyler to understand the significance of the proposed road from Newbury to Missisquoi Bay. He believed it could be the infrastructure improvement that turned the tide in Quebec. On April 15, he sent Washington the notes from Thomas Johnson, who had accompanied Osgood's Company to Metcalf's a few weeks earlier. Bayley communicated that Simon Metcalf had developed his own notes and mapwork.[124]

On April 24, the Quebec Commission entered the Champlain Valley. They stopped in Ferris Bay, near present-day Ferrisburgh on the Vermont side of Lake Champlain, home to the Ferris family. They spent the night there.[125] By April 26, Charles and John Carroll, Samuel Chase and

Benjamin Franklin was off the coast of Isle La Motte in late April 1776. *Artwork by Ashley Bowen.*

Benjamin Franklin had traveled much of the lake. They spent that night on their boats, huddled off the coast of Isle La Motte.[126] The next day, they traveled another ten miles, stopping on New York's western shore at the Point au Fer White House.[127]

At about the same time, Schuyler wrote to General Washington, expressing frustration with the pace of the boat-building effort. Originally, Congress approved funding for about one hundred new bateaux. Close to forty had been completed the previous fall. About twenty more were finished that spring, but it was difficult procuring the necessary tools and supplies to complete the rest.[128]

In one of these craft was Dr. Lewis Beebe, who traveled with his unit. He noted in his diary that with a solid wind they covered over one hundred miles to St. Jean in a single day.[129]

The Quebec Commission arrived in Montreal on April 29. While Benjamin Franklin investigated whether French Canadians would join the Revolution, Washington was moving his army from Boston to New York. While doing so, he wrote to General Bayley and made it clear the

As Benjamin Franklin and the Quebec Commission sailed north, they moved beyond this section of the Isle La Motte shoreline. *Photo by Armand Messier and Northern Vermont Aerial Photography.*

work to lay the road through the Green Mountains was to begin promptly. He confirmed that Metcalf's settlement on the Missisquoi River was an appropriate destination point.[130]

General John Thomas, who outranked Wooster, arrived at Quebec on May 2. At the same time, multiple regiments crossed the forty-fifth parallel and moved north on the Richelieu. Approximately four hundred Green Mountain Boys, along with regiments from Pennsylvania, Massachusetts, New Hampshire, Connecticut and New Jersey, moved into Quebec.[131] All of these men sailed through Alburgh and the Lake Champlain islands.

In Montreal, the commissioners met with Benedict Arnold. After being in the city for two days, they wrote to Congress and communicated the reality of the situation. Supplies, money and men were badly needed. Without them, the invasion would end in failure. On May 6, they sent a follow-up message that was even more blunt. They suggested a general retreat to save what was left of the army and urged for the fortification of the northern edge of Lake Champlain.[132] Some of this was at Arnold's insistence. He convinced them to support the construction of row galleys or gondolas at Chambly.[133]

The members were so disheartened by Wooster's attitude, inabilities and command decisions that they recommended he be replaced.[134]

George Washington, writing from New York on May 5, informed John Hancock that he had sent Jacob Bayley the necessary funds to construct the road from the Connecticut River to Missisquoi Bay. He was convinced the route would shave nearly a week's travel time for soldiers making the trek to Quebec.[135]

The resupply effort was not going as well as hoped. Elements of the Twenty-Fourth Massachusetts Regiment were in bateaux, moving over the lake. Bad weather and strong winds made boat travel unsafe, so they languished around the Lake Champlain islands for days before they resumed their journey.[136] To make matters worse, other units arrived in Chambly, having traversed the Richelieu with supplies already running low.[137] Charles Burrall's Connecticut Regiment, along with the Eighth, Fifteenth, Twenty-Fourth and Twenty-Fifth Regiments, were at near full strength but were poorly equipped.

As American forces were funneled into the theater, their worst nightmare developed at Quebec City. After months of tolerating the winter cold and weeks of trying to get healthy soldiers to participate in the siege of Quebec, British forces arrived from Europe at the end of the first week of May. Soldiers of the Crown were immediately deployed, and the American forces around the city retreated in a panic.

In Quebec Province for only two weeks, the commission members understood the gravity of the situation. Word arrived of the general retreat, and they understood that a military victory was impossible. Benjamin Franklin and Father Carroll departed Montreal and headed for St. Jean, sailing by Alburgh and Isle La Motte a few days later. As he left the area, Franklin wrote to the Continental Congress, "The army must starve, plunder, or surrender."[138] Due to the spread of the pox, over 25 percent of the men were not fit for duty.[139]

One soldier who Franklin likely intersected with while traveling south was Jeduthan Baldwin, whose engineering talents were being noticed by his commanding officers. Baldwin and 108 colonials, in four bateaux, moved past Windmill Point, north toward Île aux Noix as Franklin departed.[140]

On May 13, in the vicinity of St. Jean, some of the newly arrived American reinforcements were ordered to stop. The situation was in such disarray that many men were turned around and then sent back onto Lake Champlain. One soldier, Jonathan Hill, noted that there was a serious lack of supplies.[141]

Always one to understand threats that faced an army, Arnold grudgingly allowed an inoculation effort against smallpox on May 15. His late support was a recognition that American soldiers now faced a greater enemy than the British. He had seen the first waves grip the army and needed fresh soldiers to avoid the worst effects of the disease. However, exposing the true disarray the army faced, General John Thomas nullified the inoculation order days later.

Despite efforts to protect his men, Arnold continued to have conflicts with other officers. He ordered some private property in Montreal seized, items he believed would help the enemy war effort. Wagons of goods and supplies were taken and sent to St. Jean, where Moses Hazen was supposed to sign for them. Hazen refused to accept responsibility for the shipment.[142] The supplies were looted.

On May 20, circumstances grew worse. The army had no money to purchase desperately needed provisions from the locals. Major General John Thomas described his fighting men as destitute. He complained that the inoculation program made a large portion of his army unfit for duty.[143] He observed that the situation was deteriorating, but he believed it wasn't unsalvageable. With more units arriving from Lake Champlain, fresh soldiers that had not been ravaged by smallpox, he hoped the army could hold. Thomas believed the Richelieu River might serve as a fast, direct supply line between his forces and Ticonderoga and Crown Point. Jeduthan Baldwin, who had arrived the previous week, was still near St. Jean on May 22. The talented engineer wrote in his journal that some defensive work had been completed. However, the smallpox epidemic was getting worse, and the supply situation was borderline negligent.[144] Baldwin had participated in the army's brief inoculation program but fell very ill.

The British offensive from Quebec commenced that day. The retreating Americans put up meager resistance. To make matters worse, General Thomas contracted smallpox during the third week of May. He was soon too ill to command the army. Command fell back to the less than enthusiastic General Wooster. The remaining Quebec Commission members communicated to the Continental Congress the worsening plight of the army. They noted that smallpox seemed to be taking over the army and that many soldiers were not even getting paid. They described scant numbers of cattle being procured for the half-starved army.[145] Seeing the writing on the wall, they left Montreal. They arrived at St. Jean on May 31 and observed the disorganized, disheartened and seemingly already defeated American army.[146] In the final days of May and the first days of June, elements of the First New Jersey Regiment were crammed in bateaux and moved from Lake Champlain to the Richelieu River.[147]

General Wooster departed the army on June 1. A healthy but disgraced Wooster passed through St. Jean. There, Baldwin, who had been in Quebec for about two weeks, still suffered from smallpox. In his journal, he noted that his stomach was very sour, and he loathed trying to eat. The attending nurse recorded as many as forty pustules on his face alone.[148]

The retreating Quebec Commission members departed St. Jean the next day. They traveled south on the Richelieu to Île aux Noix, then to Alburgh's Windmill Point and finally to Pont au Fer.[149] The boat crews rowed all night until they reached the relative safety of Lake Champlain's southern areas. As they departed, Anthony Wayne's Fourth Pennsylvania Battalion arrived. Wayne would go on to become a well-known military commander, but the disintegration of the Quebec campaign was an early learning experience for him.

During this time of chaos, Simon Metcalf understood that the American effort to seize Quebec had come to a screeching halt. He dispatched a young and capable employee, Thomas Thomson, to New York and Philadelphia.[150] He worried that the American army wasn't going to pay him for the lumber he had provided. If the military couldn't pay its bills, perhaps the fledgling American government would.

The plight of the Americans got worse, not better. They were in such bad shape that they could barely organize a proper retreat. Sick men were left behind for the British to take care of. Some command-level officers simply surrendered as the enemy approached.

Montreal's location on the St. Lawrence left it hard to defend. It is west of the Richelieu River, the route many Americans used to escape. The British moved to seize the Richelieu, hoping to cut off the retreating defenders in the city. Arnold, still in command at Montreal, didn't even receive word the defenses had crumbled along the St. Lawrence.

The colonials somehow got organized enough to try a desperate attack around Three Rivers on June 7. They significantly misjudged the position and the size of the force they were about to attack. The assault was planned so that smaller units, spread throughout the forested countryside, would engage the redcoats at the same time. Companies got lost in the hours prior to the attack. The entire effort was an embarrassing disaster. The attack began, then crumbled, and the British moved in, capturing at least one general and several of his aides.[151]

For those unlucky enough to be away from the main army, smallpox decimated the ranks. Recovering near St. Jean for almost a month, Jeduthan Baldwin and others fought to survive. While the American army was routed at Three Rivers, he wrote in his journal that he still suffered from a high fever. The pox pustules were all over his body.[152] He was one of many.

By June 14, British soldiers and boats were in control of Sorel, the northernmost point of the Richelieu River.[153] The American leadership finally ordered a general retreat. Operations in Quebec had been a disaster. What was left of the army would retreat to Fort Ticonderoga and Crown Point. They would lick their wounds and retreat over the waters of the Richelieu.

The forces of the Crown moved forward, aware that the resistance in front of them was dissipating. Light infantry and grenadiers were sent south to pursue the demoralized Americans as a significant British force tried to cut off Montreal.[154]

Montreal was abandoned on June 15. When the residents of the city were not entirely enthusiastic about helping the Americans depart, Arnold threatened the Catholic clergy. He needed them to get the populace to provide wagons and bateaux necessary for the retreat.[155] Chambly was burned just in front of the British advance on June 17. The redcoats entered the northern edges of the town as the colonials departed to the south.

The lake between Rouses Point, New York, and Windmill Point in Alburgh was packed with retreating bateaux. Those streaming south were stuffed full of men, supplies and even cannon. Most traveled miles to the south, into colonial territory, and deposited their soldiers and cargo in the wilderness, still days away from Fort Ticonderoga. It was necessary, as the empty bateaux were rushed back north, to collect more elements of the army. This played out repeatedly during the final weeks of June.

The final rally point for the colonial army was the two-hundred-acre island Île aux Noix. As the crow flies, this was just a few miles from Missisquoi Bay and Metcalf's settlement. American leadership no longer wanted their army in Quebec, and Île aux Noix was an island that nobody wanted to be on. The Richelieu is shallow near the shores, with swamp-like conditions. It is a prime breeding ground for mosquitos and other bugs, which greedily fed on the defeated Americans.

Bayze Wells, who scouted these critically important regions in 1775, was now also recovering from smallpox. His unit was ordered to Île aux Noix on June 16. About 1,500 infantrymen had already arrived, most of them sick. The infected and exhausted men had few blankets, and the weather was quite wet.[156]

Boats moved north and south above and below the island. The evacuation of St. Jean was underway, with the bateaux trying to get everyone out. The British, advancing from the north, were only hours behind the Americans. Their scouting parties took advantage of the chaos of the retreat. On June 17, a party of natives ambushed soldiers from the Sixth Pennsylvania Regiment near Île aux Noix. They had been fishing, trying to feed the army. The natives killed and scalped four men and took six prisoners. The survivors solemnly buried their fallen comrades on the island.[157]

A logjam of sorts developed at Île aux Noix. By June 18, thousands of troops were on the island, over two thousand now infected with smallpox. There were still six hundred troops at St. Jean, deployed to slow the advancing British. Even some of this rear guard became part of the general retreat. While packed bateaux rowed south, groups of soldiers retreated along the shorelines.[158] Meanwhile, Schuyler wrote to authorities in New Hampshire, asking them to get more soldiers to the Onion River as soon as possible.[159]

Finally, the last Americans left St. Jean and torched the fort. Arnold and his lieutenants rode north to confirm the location of the enemy approach. British columns were in sight, and even Arnold was convinced the situation was hopeless. They withdrew and rushed to the final departing boats. Arnold shot his own horse so the British wouldn't find and use it. The last bateau to abandon St. Jean carried Arnold; Jeduthan Baldwin, who had finally recovered from smallpox; and a few other soldiers. They arrived at Île aux Noix around midnight. Baldwin wrote in his journal that he slept in the bateau, not even going on the island that night.[160]

The soldiers on Île aux Noix were dying in disturbing numbers. Surgeon Samuel Merrick wrote that his boat had been one of the last to leave St. Jean. When his party arrived on the island, unmoving bodies littered the shoreline. Others begged for help, unable to go any farther. The surgeons had no medical supplies with which to treat the sick men; those supplies had already been ordered south.[161] The few doctors, with no further options for care, pitched their tents, shut the flaps and avoided the terminally ill. Americans had been left to die on the ground. Some boats were heading south onto Lake Champlain full of smallpox-infected soldiers.

Smallpox was not the only menace to those remaining on Île aux Noix. Mistakes, accidents, selfish survival instincts and the enemy stalked the exposed force. One captain walked outside the perimeter, looking for sentries posted on the outskirts of the island. In the darkness, they mistook him for an enemy soldier and shot him through the heart.[162] In another instance, a unit procured a fresh supply of beef. They hungrily devoured it, greedily not sharing with others. There were no supplies, and fresh, clean water was nearly nonexistent. Soldiers had to drink from standing water on the low-lying island or directly from the waters of the Richelieu River. For days, soldiers had been defecating and urinating wherever they could, creating unsanitary conditions. Drinking the water there only increased the illnesses savaging the army. For a few days, those men lived in their own waste.

Dr. Lewis Beebe recorded the state of the troops in his journal on the afternoon he arrived. As night settled on one of the longest days of the year, the cries and groans of those lying on the ground took the place of the evening crickets. He wrote about a large barn where scores of very sick men, some with maggots oozing out of their wounds, were housed. Many died; some still clung to life.[163] Beebe's service there was mercifully short, as he departed for Crown Point after a short time.

Captain John Lacey of Pennsylvania also kept a dairy. He recorded some of the most graphic imagery of the hellhole that had become the American army's position on Île aux Noix. At least two large pits were dug and served as mass graves. Upward of twenty soldiers died each day, their skin covered

A smallpox outbreak decimated the American army in Quebec. The exhausted and ill soldiers retreated to the west of Alburgh and the Lake Champlain islands. *Artwork by Ashley Bowen.*

with lumpy pock wounds, with flies, lice and other bugs infesting the open soars. The corpses were dumped on top of one another in the pits. When one pit was full, another was dug.[164]

Jeduthan Baldwin departed with other soldiers on June 20. Several members of his regiment succumbed to illness during the retreat. That night, he and his traveling companions stayed on the east side of Lake Champlain, probably somewhere just south of Windmill Point in Alburgh.[165]

By Friday, June 21, the number of soldiers on the island was finally diminishing. Supplies were scarce. Captain Charles Cushing reported that there was only dried pork to eat and that the remaining men had run out of flour.

It is not known to what extent the smallpox epidemic at Île aux Noix affected the Missisquoi Abenaki. It is doubtful their old village on the banks of the Missisquoi even remained inhabited with the fighting so close. With scouting parties, raiders and entire armies so close to Missisquoi Bay, they sought the safety of places like Odanak or Coos near the Connecticut River.

The British were energized by their success and the American collapse. As they settled in at St. Jean, they witnessed the last of the American bateaux desperately retreating.[166] With the threat removed from Quebec, plans were put in place to retake the Champlain Valley. Even prior to the enemy withdrawal, bateaux flowed southward over the Richelieu. The infrastructure was being put in place to construct ships to retake Crown Point and Ticonderoga.

On the night of the summer solstice, the shortest night of the year, the remaining Americans departed the Richelieu and entered the slightly wider confines of northern Lake Champlain. The men in the bateaux desperately rowed south. In some cases, commanders didn't know where their units were. Others, forced to wait for more boats at Alburgh or Isle La Motte, feared an imminent attack.

Baldwin recorded on the first day of summer that he crossed the lake to Point au Fer and ate breakfast with other officers. During the day, they fell back to Isle La Motte. As spring turned to summer, he ate supper on the island with the rest of the defeated American army.[167]

Chapter 5

"CRITICAL MONTHS"

Summer of 1776

On June 22, much of the force remained on Isle La Motte. General Sullivan, one of the many command-level officers attempting to deal with the situation, feared smallpox might remove what was left of the army while the British organized an assault.[168] He was also concerned that the enemy was not far behind. Twelve English soldiers and thirty natives, traveling the Richelieu in birch-bark canoes, investigated the land near Île aux Noix and came upon the rear guard of the American army, a small unit captained by James Wilson. After an exchange of musket fire, the Americans were overwhelmed and Captain Wilson surrendered. British casualties included one native killed and a few men wounded.[169] The English army was now on the Quebec border.

On the twenty-fourth, General Sullivan wrote to George Washington that twenty to sixty soldiers each day were falling to smallpox. He desperately hoped the British would not attack and urgently needed the bateaux to return to take his men south. He penned another letter to Schuyler, suggesting fortifying Windmill Point or Point au Fer. Sullivan realized that the eastern shore near present-day Alburgh was infested with enemy soldiers. Some of his men left their bateau and went ashore. Gunfire soon erupted in the distance. Bands of natives, allied to the English, roamed the woods around the American army.[170] The colonials realized they wouldn't have time to fortify Windmill Point. Desperate for intelligence, Ensign Hughes was dispatched around Isle La Motte to look out for the enemy and maintain contact with other colonial scouts.[171]

Above: Parts of the American army retreated through Alburgh in late June 1776. *Photo by Armand Messier and Northern Vermont Aerial Photography.*

Opposite: As the Americans fled Quebec, they camped on Isle La Motte in June 1776. *Artwork by Lindsay DiDio.*

While the battered and bruised army waited to be rescued, Sullivan prepared for the inevitable. The British would be coming. He ordered upgrades and better fortifications to be completed on the White House on Point au Fer. Sparse groups of healthy soldiers created a cedar post fence around the structure and erected a covered walkway from the shoreline to the main building. The men were ordered to find cannon to improve the defenses.[172]

Sadly, there were still Americans on Île aux Noix, waiting for boats. British scouts already operated farther south, and the men risked being cut off. The remaining one thousand soldiers crossed the Richelieu River and retreated over land. They snuck through the thick woods of Quebec just north of the forty-fifth parallel, then managed to reach northern Alburgh. British, Tory and native bands were right behind them. Americans inched south along the town's western shore with nervous looks to the north. After a frantic retreat that lasted more than a day, they waded through shallow water and arrived on Isle La Motte.[173] A separate group had proceeded by land on the western shore and arrived at Point au Fer.[174]

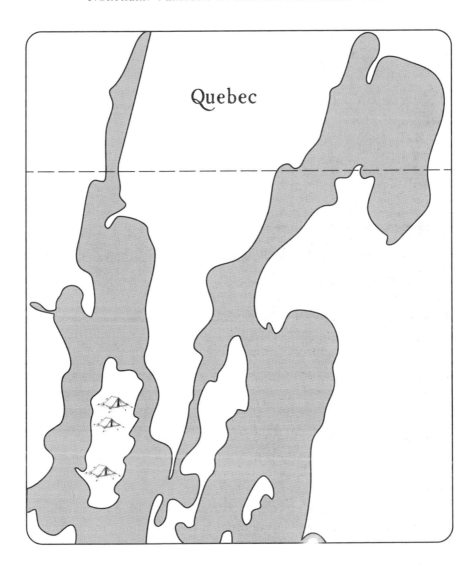

On June 25, distant from the Champlain Valley, George Washington responded to Jacob Bayley in Newbury. Washington was taking in the shifting reality, and after months of planning, the road from the Connecticut River across the Green Mountains was suddenly no longer an asset. Colonel Bayley's people had cleared a path of trees more than fifteen feet wide, and scout teams had marked most of the rest of the route. The American presence in Quebec had evaporated. Now there was the threat of the British sweeping down the lake without opposition. Washington could not risk the possibility that the road would facilitate

American commanders fortified the position at Point au Fer in Upstate New York. *Photo by Armand Messier and Northern Vermont Aerial Photography.*

There were not enough boats for the fleeing Americans. Several companies had to wade through shallow water between Isle La Motte and Alburgh to escape the British. *Photo by Armand Messier and Northern Vermont Aerial Photography.*

England's counterattack and threaten southern New England. Ultimately, he left the continuation of the project up to Bayley but communicated that some resources were being reallocated for defensive measures.[175]

On June 26, the last rescue caravan of bateaux departed Crown Point for points north. The final elements of the colonial army, stranded on Isle La Motte, could finally escape. The soldiers waiting for rescue were sick with either malaria or smallpox, or both, and some died before the boats arrived. All, whether healthy or sick, were dangerously exposed to the enemy.

The fleet of bateaux arrived and picked up the shattered remnants, but the nightmare wasn't over. Unfortunately, they brought their ailments and illnesses back with them. Captain Lacy of Pennsylvania observed that the journey over Lake Champlain was particularly grim. While resting on an island, he wrote in his journal that the boats overflowed with sick and exhausted soldiers. He estimated that ten men per day died while traveling the lake. His unit didn't reach Crown Point until July 1, suggesting that disease took another fifty lives as the men rowed away from the British.[176]

Another soldier, John Greenwood, also scribbled in his journal during a moment of rest on one of Lake Champlain's tiny islands. He noted that the boat stopped around noon, and the men divided up their meager food supplies. They hastily cooked their pork rations on a piece of bark and hungrily ingested dirt and rice with their meal.[177]

North of the forty-fifth parallel, the British settled in. The length of Lake Champlain separated the British and the Americans, and they needed a navy to challenge the *Enterprise* and *Liberty*. Chambly and Fort St. Jean became hubs of activity, with Île aux Noix used as a forward-operating base. The little island once again swarmed with activity. It was within striking distance of Missisquoi Bay and allowed them to control the entrance to the Richelieu River. Plans for a substantial outpost began almost as soon as the Americans left.

For the rebel sympathizers residing in Upstate New York and the New Hampshire Grants, the retreat brought fears that organized Tory groups might coalesce and fight for the Crown.[178] During the previous fighting season, successes by revolutionaries quelled Tory sympathizers from taking an active role in the conflict. Communications between English forces in Quebec and southern citizens still allied with the king had already been intercepted—by colonial forces. Whispers and rumors of different allegiances polluted the countryside. Militias prepared to be called up. In June, Gideon Brownson's unit was organized and served within the New

Hampshire Grants. The Allen family was involved; Ebenezer Allen signed on for a thirty-day deployment.[179]

American leadership understood the dire situation, and George Washington focused on ways to slow the British advance. Soon, his view shifted definitively on the road through the Green Mountains. He suggested that Bayley delay the entire project.[180] To add to the tension, intelligence surfaced that the British might construct a road from St. Jean to Missisquoi Bay.[181]

Meanwhile, Simon Metcalf sent his right-hand man, Thomas Thomson, to Philadelphia to deliver bills totaling $750 for lumber delivered to St. Jean during the fall invasion of 1775.[182] Congress accepted the bill but did not move forward with payment. While Thomson was on this mission, Metcalf and several of his people worked along the Onion River. He assessed the land and wanted to purchase oxen, cows and farm supplies for his settlement at Prattsburgh. He was extremely unlucky. He found himself among retreating American soldiers, some of whom had concerns about his past dealings with Quebec. Even though Metcalf had completed his business and was about to return to Prattsburgh, his presence raised the ire of the defeated army. Colonial soldiers stole his newly purchased farm animals, arrested his workmen, seized his boats and had him imprisoned.[183]

The army had retreated safely to the southern reaches of the lake, but American leadership desperately needed information. An unnamed American lieutenant led a team of four scouts back up to St. Jean to gather information. The men became separated, but two of them made it to the Missisquoi River and returned to the American lines.[184] With so many enemy soldiers deployed there, they were not able to collect much intelligence.

By July 3, the American army was quartered at Crown Point, Chimney Point and Fort Ticonderoga. At the northern end of the lake, the defenses at the Point au Fer White House were completed, and those men rejoined the rest of the army.[185]

A race was on to see which side could assemble a navy fast enough to control the Champlain Valley. The British had the best navy in the world, and their work involved bringing together a fleet that would brush aside anything the Americans might cobble together. More reinforcements were on the way from England, but the small rebel navy had to be dealt with.

The Americans now had a respectable defensive position well away from the enemy, but controlling the lake was not going to be easy. Their own reinforcements were coming up from the other colonies. Work began on the Vermont side of the lake, involving the construction of an entirely new fort across from Fort Ticonderoga. It was dubbed Mount Independence.

A significant colonial force was also at Crown Point, but smallpox still ravaged the men. One estimate had the number of sick men at five hundred. A decision was made to evacuate all the sick to Chimney Point, on the Vermont side of the lake. The healthy soldiers remained at Crown Point. There, the difficult task of re-forming a defeated army began.[186]

The shipbuilding effort became a major focus for the opposing forces. The British began constructing large vessels at St. Jean. They also disassembled some of their ships on the St. Lawrence River in Quebec, floated and portaged their hulls over the Richelieu River and began reconstructing them. For the Americans, Benedict Arnold was put in charge of assembling a fleet that might stand against the most powerful navy in the world. It was an impossible task, but Arnold's building of the Lake Champlain fleet ranks among the most important events of the Revolutionary War.

American commanders needed to keep tabs on activity to the north. On July 5, approximately two hundred colonial soldiers departed for Cumberland Head to investigate British movement south of the forty-fifth parallel.[187] As intelligence filtered in, they made a determination that severely impacted the northern end of the lake. Metcalf's sawmill, which had supported the invasion of Quebec just months before, was too close to British forces. The enemy could not be allowed to take advantage of such infrastructure in Missisquoi Bay. The Americans might be able to limit enemy operations within the Richelieu River, but to the east, Metcalf's sawmill could not be permitted to support the British shipbuilding effort.

In the middle of July, after Simon Metcalf had been taken from the Onion River and his assets seized, he was released by the Americans. Metcalf was free to return to the Missisquoi River and resume his life. However, his money, his workmen and his farm animals were not returned. He procured transport on the lake and returned to Missisquoi.[188]

General Horatio Gates, the new overall commander of the American effort on Lake Champlain, decided that Metcalf's sawmill had to be destroyed. Portions of Seth Warner's regiment were stationed at the advance post of Crown Point during the first weeks of July, and Gates wanted his men to torch Metcalf's mill. However, large portions of Warner's detachment were already spread thin, scouting up and down New York, the Lake Champlain islands and the western Green Mountains. An officer present at Crown Point, Captain Gideon Brownson, responded to Gates that Warner's men were already assigned to other duties. Brownson suggested that Colonel Wait's men were available for the task.[189] Events were set in motion that would bring the war to Missisquoi Bay.

Gates called Arnold, Sullivan and the rest of his generals to Crown Point on July 7. They debated how best to blunt the expected British advance. Crown and Chimney Points, located approximately thirteen miles north of Ticonderoga, was made an advance lookout post for the army. Ticonderoga and Mount Independence were deemed the most appropriate locations to conduct defensive operations.[190] The smallpox patients at Crown Point and Chimney Point were evacuated to avoid contact with fresh soldiers arriving at Fort Ticonderoga. The ailing men were removed to fortifications around Lake George, New York.

Gates still wanted to eliminate Metcalf's sawmill but had to postpone the plan until the right force was available. Colonel Wait's men were well acquainted with the eastern side of the lake and had already been on scouting missions along the border. On July 9, Dr. Lewis Beebe scribbled an entry in his journal, noting that Wait's men had returned to base in numerous bateaux and had several native prisoners, possibly Abenaki, with them.[191]

At some point in July, General Carleton and the British commanders became aware of the extent of engineering and roadwork begun earlier through the Green Mountains. Loyalist informants revealed that nearly two-thirds of one road had been completed. It stretched from the area of Coos on the Connecticut River, near Jacob Bayley's settlements, all the way to the Lamoille River in central Vermont. Even more concerning were reports that the Americans had started on a route from the Onion River to Missisquoi Bay. The British came to understand that their own work to broaden the road from Île aux Noix to Missisquoi Bay, using the small River de Sud, could actually be used by the Americans at some point.[192] It put an emphasis on regaining control of Lake Champlain.

During the second and third weeks of July, the Americans struggled with how to control the area. Colonel Hurd, writing reports from the Connecticut River, described scouting missions by Captain Paine to the north. Thirty or more miles of road were complete, and he thought Metcalf's plans for the rest of the project were still viable.[193] A total of 110 men had been involved with the engineering as far north as Peacham.[194] A blockhouse had also been erected in that town. It was designed to serve as a defensive location if the workers ever came under attack.[195]

On July 14, an ambitious colonial scout named Benjamin Whitcomb received orders to take command of a team of three other American soldiers. They were ordered to Quebec on a scouting mission. Three days later, Whitcomb's group was near the Onion River, where severe storms hindered their advance through the woods. It rained so hard that they stopped and waited out the winds, the downpours and the thunder and lightning. At about the same time, on the east side of the mountains, Colonel Bayley received orders from the New Hampshire chain of command. He was to redirect men from the road project to collect intelligence from the area of Lake Memphremagog down to the Onion River.[196]

By July 20, Whitcomb's scouting unit was at the northern edge of Lake Champlain, near Missisquoi Bay.[197] They passed through Colonel Wait's two-hundred-man unit operating at the mouth of the Onion River. Wait was the northern edge of the army and felt dangerously exposed.[198]

Further small-scale activity continued near the border. General Sullivan was satisfied with the work at Point au Fer and believed it allowed the colonials to defend the northern reaches.[199] On the other side of the lake, Simon Metcalf was finally back in his settlement. The journey had taken him by the Point au Fer defenses, and he believed the British would need to engage that position before moving toward the broader lake. When home, he sat down and penned a letter to his closest colonial ally, Jacob Bayley. He described the events of the previous few weeks. Metcalf also hosted unwelcome and dangerous visitors. Four Canadians who claimed to have served in James Livingston's regiment during the Quebec invasion stopped by his settlement. They said they had information valuable to the American cause and reported that the British were already bringing larger boats up the Chambly rapids.[200] Metcalf, wary of his very recent entanglement with the colonials, sent the four Frenchmen from Canada south and then east through the woods, on the path to Jacob Bayley. The Canadian informants and their knowledge of enemy operations were very important. If the British were already attempting to bring their larger craft from the St. Lawrence on to Lake Champlain, that was grim news.

The Americans had more scout missions underway in addition to Benjamin Whitcomb's. Captain Wilson arrived with his unit on the eastern shore of Isle La Motte on July 22. His focus was to the east, investigating the channel between Alburgh, North Hero and into Maquam Bay. His men detained a Frenchman in a canoe. They tried to communicate, but none of the unit spoke French. They next interviewed another traveler, John Davie. Wilson was not satisfied with any of the answers he'd been given. He ordered the men transported south with Lieutenant Clark.[201] Clark's report to Colonel Hartley, the commanding officer of Crown Point, was bad news for Simon Metcalf. Clark argued that Metcalf and others living at his settlement should be detained.[202] They were living too close to the enemy's sphere of influence, were too far away from the American lines and should be arrested to prevent collaboration with the British.

Both the Americans and the British badly needed information. The British, trying to bring part of their strong navy to bear, wanted to know what they were up against. The Americans, fearing the enemy could bring together a sizable fleet, needed to know how fast that force was being constructed. Spy missions went up and down the valley.

On July 25, Lieutenant Whitcomb crossed into Quebec to gather information and harass the British. In the coming days, he got a good glimpse of the shipbuilding activities at St. Jean and wounded British general James Gordon in a sniper ambush. He was pursued but eluded capture.[203]

In late July, Captains Stevens and Bigelow led approximately eighty colonial soldiers north to Île aux Noix. They carried a flag of truce and were under orders to deliver chests of clothing and supplies for two American officers held by the British. When they arrived, there were about fifty regulars working on the island. They coolly respected the flag of truce and waited for a larger group of reinforcements to arrive from St. Jean. Ultimately, they demanded that the Americans surrender. The British were extremely angry because of Whitcomb's recent attack. General Gordon was dying, so the British honored the flag of truce but took the Americans captive.[204]

By July 27, the Frenchmen that Metcalf had directed through the Green Mountains arrived in Newbury. They told their stories again, providing valuable intelligence. Bayley sent scouting missions west, trying to keep tabs on the Onion River.[205] One of these involved providing escorts for the four Frenchmen.[206] Bayley felt the intelligence was worth moving up the chain of command. These missions operated in areas where the British were feared to have Tory spies and their own scouting missions. General Gates communicated as much to General Washington in a letter on July 29. His staff feared that the British might attack through Missisquoi Bay and the Onion River.[207]

By the first week of August, the Americans were still trying to gather information from the eastern side of the Green Mountains. Scouting parties traveled up the Connecticut River and looked for enemy activity around Lake Memphremagog. One mission had soldiers embark toward Metcalf's to keep him updated on the movement of American scouts along the border.[208] Another scout team operated on the Lamoille River, looking for British raiding parties.[209]

On August 6, Gates learned of the intelligence from the Frenchmen who had been at Metcalf's. They told the general that large numbers of Hessian soldiers were now in Quebec. However, they mentioned that some of the mercenaries, far from their German homelands, were deserting daily. They let Gates know that four Hessians had arrived at Metcalf's just a few days prior as they departed. Gates immediately wanted to take advantage of this information and sent out a force to retrieve the deserters at Missisquoi.[210]

On August 6, Colonel Benjamin Whitcomb finally returned to Fort Ticonderoga.[211] Whitcomb had been in the northern reaches for weeks. While the American leadership weighed its information about the British, the residents of the Onion River became more nervous. They signed a letter to the leadership at Ticonderoga. Colonel Warner's regiment was supposed to provide protection, but his men had been called on to perform other duties.[212] The residents argued that it was harvest time, and they feared for their crops.

In war there is no rest for the weary. Whitcomb received orders to go to Missisquoi Bay, visit Metcalf's and retrieve the Hessian deserters. The wind conditions were nearly perfect, and he retrieved one Hessian, a Captain Mesnard, and brought him to the American camps in short order. The mission corrected a piece of bad intelligence, as apparently there had been just one deserter. However, Mesnard stated that there were likely sixty or seventy Hessians roaming the woods of Quebec. Most of them were trying to get away from the coming battles. Whitcomb's official report didn't mention any interactions with Metcalf, his workers or anyone else in Missisquoi Bay.

While it might never be known for certain, it is very likely that Metcalf's sawmill was torched during Whitcomb's mission. When Whitcomb retrieved the deserter, he also might have been acting on the earlier orders from Gates to destroy the sawmill. The evidence for this is only circumstantial, but there was plenty of action around Metcalf's settlement in late July and early August. To that point, the heartbeat of the settlement, the sawmill, was still in existence. Benjamin Whitcomb retrieved the Hessian on August 7 or 8, and the sawmill was spoken of in the past tense after that.

Two versions of the fate of the mill have been told, both probably containing some element of truth. The first is that it was taken out by two colonial soldiers who came through the woods from outposts in the southern Green Mountains. Thomas Butterfield, a man who resettled in Swanton after the Revolutionary War, may have been one of the soldiers. In this account, the Allen clan was all too happy to order the burning of a mill, as it was associated with New York's claims to Vermont.[213] It is possible that the Allens were aware of General Gates's orders and approved of the measure.

The other account involves colonial soldiers, one of whom was Robert Coffrin, arriving through the woods near the Missisquoi River. They, too, had journeyed from the south-central part of the state. In this version, Coffrin confronted Metcalf at his door and informed him that the mill needed to be taken out to prevent it from being used by the enemy. Metcalf argued but did not interfere as the colonial soldiers put the torch to his mill.[214] Robert Coffrin had enlisted in the First New Hampshire Regiment in 1776.[215] Thomas Butterfield enlisted in the same unit at about the same time. While these versions can be logically woven into the sequence of events of the summer of 1776, they do not appear to match Metcalf's personal belief that it was the British who burned his sawmill.[216]

It is possible, with all the frayed loyalties in the region, that the British became aware of the colonial use of the settlement. Metcalf had housed disloyal French habitants, deserting Hessians and colonial scouts. The British may have also learned that Metcalf sold goods to the colonials during the 1775 Quebec invasion. These would have been provocation enough for the location to be neutralized. However, it does support their interest in the coming British invasion of Lake Champlain. They had ships and men massing at St. Jean and Île aux Noix. With the war raging, they could have made use of a valuable sawmill on the border.

Around August 7, British commanders officially told Captains Stevens and Biglow and their men why they had been held for two weeks. They decreed that the assassination of General Gordon was an unacceptable incident, well beyond the rules of war.[217] It is not clear if they knew that Benjamin Whitcomb was responsible. Grudgingly respecting the flag of truce, they released the Americans. On the same day, American colonel Hurd, operating along the Connecticut River, wrote a letter to the leadership of New Hampshire. Another scout had come in from Missisquoi Bay. Hurd communicated that he distrusted some of the information provided by Simon Metcalf.[218]

Once Metcalf's sawmill was burned, American leadership wondered if the act had turned him against the Revolution. On August 9, Metcalf's two associates, Mr. Thomson and Anthony Gerard, arrived near Crown Point in a canoe. Their long journey through the colonies representing Metcalf's interest was finally complete.

Metcalf had contacted Jacob Bayley earlier that summer about ensuring the safe return of the two men. However, they were seized and searched, and the Americans feared they were spies. The two men offered their papers, documents associated with Metcalf's business dealings and private letters.

Metcalf's sawmill was burned in early August 1776. *Artwork by Ashley Bowen.*

The Americans were unconvinced and concerned that they might be letting spies return to Quebec. The men were held and temporarily jailed. About $500 was confiscated.[219]

Just a few days later, Bayley believed everything was fine at Metcalf's. He wrote to Gates and wanted to know if any more Hessians had defected through Missisquoi Bay. He didn't indicate that he knew the sawmill was no longer in operation. Bayley ordered a man to serve in Missisquoi Bay to keep tabs on the enemy to the north.[220] The Newbury commander had not given up on the recently abandoned road. He reminded Gates that the first thirty miles were done and that, if needed, cattle could be driven through the existing trail.

On August 11, Colonel Hartley, one of the officers at Crown Point, wrote to General Gates about the return of Metcalf's associates. It was a minor point in the correspondence, but Hartley referred to Metcalf's sawmill as having been burned.[221]

The British moved to solidify their hold on the Richelieu River on August 14. Elements of the Fifty-Third Regiment of Foot, including Lieutenant William Digby, arrived at Île aux Noix just days after the burning of Metcalf's sawmill. They were accompanied by bands of natives, who protected the wooded areas on either side of the island. Digby noted in his journal that the island was muddy from recent rains.[222] Classic New England summer thunderstorms blanketed the Champlain Valley for several days. Digby's men experienced intensely hot and humid days and almost constant storms. It rained so hard that soldiers thought the island might flood. In the first hours after their arrival, it rained all night. The tents provided little protection. An advanced post was established about four miles below Île aux Noix, on the mainland. The soldiers reported that there were great packs of wolves and wild dogs howling at night.[223]

By the second week of August, the British had turned St. Jean into a fully operational naval base. The English navy grew substantially each week. They finalized their plans for Île aux Noix and prepared upgrades on the island. Scores of British soldiers, French *habitants*, Hessian mercenaries, native allies and other Loyalists descended on the island in early August. The men began construction on a multipurpose base.[224] They deepened, reinforced and expanded the twenty-year-old entrenchments constructed during the French and Indian War. Specific care went into redesigning the layout to prevent soldiers from being hit if American vessels reached the narrows of the Richelieu.

All the hard work that Benedict Arnold had put into building the fleet came to fruition as the British gathered just a few miles away. The first part of the American fleet was near Point au Fer as the British fortified Île aux Noix.

The British were not done assuring their access to the waters of Lake Champlain. They continued plans to improve the portage trail that Simon Metcalf established in the early 1770s. He had used it to get lumber and goods back and forth between his property and the Richelieu River. The British now used it to move scouts onto Missisquoi Bay. As they thought about expanding its use, one proposal was to use one hundred French *habitant* workers with axes. They could widen the route and be done in about two days.[225]

Despite all the activity around Île aux Noix, they were unable to prevent American scouts from collecting information. John Brown, who had surveyed the area the previous fall, operated clandestinely on the eastern side of the lake. He was in the vicinity of St. Jean and Île aux Noix for several days. When Brown tried to return, he was discovered by natives and pursued through the woods north of Missisquoi Bay. He eluded them, found the bay's north shore and contacted the American ships operating to the south.[226]

Metcalf's life had already been upended. It was about to get worse. During the last week of August, from his settlement on the Missisquoi, Metcalf heard significant cannon fire. He put his ear to the wind and suspected it came from the northwest, likely Île aux Noix. He decided to investigate, leaving his wife, child and remaining workers behind. Crossing Missisquoi Bay, he heard the British regulars and French work crews expanding the portage between the bay and the Richelieu River. He was seized by natives and taken prisoner to St. Jean.[227]

As the British prepared to move south, they sent their own scout teams over Lake Champlain during the last week of August. Around August 28, raiding parties operated in Maquam Bay and near the Onion River. The Americans avoided a confrontation, but British and Indian operatives burned the homes of at least nine separate families.[228] A few days later and a bit farther south, Colonel Joseph Wait evaluated the colonial defensive positions along the Onion River. He thought the best location was Remember Baker's blockhouse in present-day Winooski. As he surveyed the land, he thought a detachment could occupy Colchester Point. He believed men could be stationed in Jericho, farther back along the Onion River, as well.[229] He filed a report, and the American generals ordered Captain Faucett's company, already operating in the area, to maintain the position.[230]

At the end of August, the British prepared for their push south, and Île aux Noix became a staging area. Elements of the Twenty-Ninth Regiment were sent down in the final days of the month.[231] Other units were stationed there as well. By the end of the first week of September, British forces were still gathering north of Missisquoi Bay and Windmill Point. The remaining elements of the Twenty-Ninth Regiment moved to St. Jean.[232] Other units were on their way as well. Blockhouses had been erected in different locations on the island. These structures were two stories high, had defensive cannons placed on the inside and housed as many as two hundred soldiers.[233]

After weeks of tension and uncertainty regarding a larger engagement, the first shots were fired on the evening of September 2. Arnold's little fleet had grown, and more boats were sailing north. The vessels had made it to Cumberland Head, just offshore of present-day Plattsburgh. When his men spied a group of approximately twenty enemy soldiers on the shore, their muskets were primed to unleash a quick volley. Arnold fired grapeshot and scattered the small force. A group of colonials went ashore to gather information, but the enemy was gone.[234]

Events escalated on September 3. The tiny American fleet was anchored off of Isle La Motte that evening.[235] Benjamin Whitcomb and four others

Benedict Arnold had his American fleet off the southern coast of Isle La Motte in early September 1776. *Photo by Armand Messier and Northern Vermont Aerial Photography.*

were unleashed yet again, this time in a birch-bark canoe. Their orders were to investigate enemy activity north of Île aux Tetes, just south of Île aux Noix. Another group, commanded by Ensign McCoy and including Ensign Stiles and two others, was released around Alburgh. They had strict orders to not engage the enemy but to get as close to their installations as possible and observe. Finally, Arnold employed a local Frenchman to go above the border and bring back any useful information.

Arnold, hoping to prevent the British from sailing into Lake Champlain, stationed his group of vessels just north of Windmill Point. He positioned them in a line, hoping to display strength and defiance so close to the enemy positions. At this point, the fleet consisted of nine ships: the schooners *Royal Savage, Liberty* and *Revenge*; the sloop *Enterprise*; and five gunboats. Arnold, in a typical display of boldness, sent another bateau into the narrows of the Richelieu River within a mile of British occupied Île aux Tetes.[236] The scout boat witnessed several hundred Canadians and Indians.[237] Arnold, not afraid to invite conflict, had his smaller craft scour the inner coastlines, including every small bay and hidden cove, looking for any positional advantage if the enemy journeyed south.

Arnold suspected that the recently constructed British fleet was close and knew enemy agents were even closer. Operating from Île aux Noix and Île

The American gunboat *Boston* was off the coast of Windmill Point in Alburgh prior to the Battle of Valcour Island. *Artwork by Josh Sinz.*

aux Tetes, English scouting parties, augmented by Canadian militia and Indians, had already infiltrated the woods on the New York and Vermont shores of Lake Champlain. Eighteen men from the *Boston* went ashore near Windmill Point to gather wood to construct fascines, obstructions placed along the hull of vessels meant to protect sailors from gunfire. They encountered an enemy force of more than twice their size, and there was a short battle on the Alburgh shoreline. Two Americans were killed and seven wounded.[238] A British lieutenant ordered the Americans to surrender. In a replay of what happened at Cumberland Head, the American fleet sprayed the coast of Alburgh with grapeshot, scattering the enemy force.[239] Search parties were sent inland. A button and a hat from the Forty-Seventh Regiment were found. With two engagements from either side of the coast, Arnold felt too exposed and ordered the fleet south.

Not all of the intrigue centered on naval activity, however. During the first week of September, another Hessian soldier was brought in by the Americans. Anthony Fasselabend, who had recently been deployed to Quebec, confirmed reports that large numbers of the Hessian soldiers had already deserted.[240]

On the night of September 6, Arnold's fleet was off the northwest coast of Isle La Motte, where the water is particularly shallow. If confronted by a superior number of British vessels moving south, Arnold's gunboats could maneuver well, as their hulls did not have a deep draft. Some of the enemy ships were much larger and would not have been able to maneuver in shallow waters. Additionally, if overwhelmed, the American boats had two means of escape. The main channel to the west offered a quick getaway. East of Isle La Motte, running along Alburgh's west coast, was another viable route of escape. After dark, while Arnold waited for the English fleet to appear, nobody detected the approach of a single birch-bark canoe. English lieutenant Scott and several natives were onboard. The craft wove through the American fleet, looking for an opportunity to seize a prisoner. When that opportunity did not arise, it traveled farther south, beyond the American ships.[241] On September 7, Arnold dispatched Benjamin Whitcomb yet again, this time on the western side of the lake.[242] In his regular communications with the commanding generals at Crown Point and Ticonderoga, Arnold disclosed that he had deployed guard boats operating near Missisquoi Bay. He did not want the British to surprise his fleet from that direction.[243]

The nervous Americans attempted to assess how far south the British land forces had moved. They studied the coast of New York. They analyzed the Isle La Motte and Alburgh shorelines and watched for movement. As they waited and watched, the American fleet was augmented by two more vessels. The gondola *New Jersey* arrived, then the cutter *Lee*.[244] Arnold hoped the newer vessels would add significant punching ability to his assorted vessels.

Their arrival helped, but the Americans knew that pressure was building along the coastlines. Arnold continued to dispatch scout ships north to keep a watchful eye on Windmill Point. The enemy needed to pass that location, and he hoped to collect the teams of scouts sent out earlier. His vessels soon reported voices coming from the woods. Next, they heard the sounds of axes felling trees. The Americans feared the British were clearing paths and setting up artillery near the coast. This seriously endangered the fleet. The colonials pulled back once again. On September 8, the fleet moved back to the southern tip of Isle La Motte.[245]

Benedict Arnold brought his fleet to the northern coast of Isle La Motte. *Photo by Armand Messier and Northern Vermont Aerial Photography.*

The next day brought more reinforcements, with the gondola *New York* pulling into the line. Intelligence arrived pertaining to the border, and it was not good news. Stiles and McCoy returned and reported that the Richelieu River was bustling with activity. They had been to St. Jean and witnessed scores of British regulars. At least thirty-four large birch-bark canoes carrying approximately six hundred natives had already moved south. The men reported that the British navy was preparing to look for the American fleet. At least twenty enemy tents were camped on Hospital Island, just above the border.

Arnold pushed for more information. The Frenchman Anthony Gerard was back living on his own property. As circumstances would have it, he could not escape the path of the war. The American guard boats in Missisquoi Bay noticed that Gerard was in the area. The Frenchman was on an errand for Catherine Metcalf, who still lived at the Metcalf residence on the Missisquoi River. It had been nearly two weeks since her husband had departed. She had called on Gerard, who had worked for the family for some time, to investigate. His first stop had been the home of another Frenchman, a Mr. Thomas, who lived in Alburgh, or present-day North Hero. Gerard had only started to look for Metcalf when the

American guard boats seized him.[246] Gerard described himself as living with Metcalf, but this was probably a reference to working on Metcalf's property. The American scouts reported his presence to Arnold, who had never seen the report indicating suspicions about him at Ticonderoga earlier in the summer. Arnold wanted intelligence, and Gerard jumped at the opportunity for further employment. The general sent him on a recon mission through Missisquoi Bay. He was supposed to return in four days' time with news about the British strength at Île aux Noix.[247]

On or around September 16, the Frenchman returned with a lot of information. He confirmed what the Americans suspected: there were thousands of Hessians and British soldiers stationed at various installations along the Richelieu. Large numbers were uncomfortably close, at Île aux Noix. Also, Gerard reported that Metcalf was being held at St. Jean. Arnold believed the information valuable, but Gerard carried a conspicuous safe passage pass from a British officer. He was arrested and ferried off to the American forts to the south.[248] In his report, Arnold described Gerard's residence as "opposite Isle La Motte," suggesting the Frenchman's home was on the eastern shore of Alburgh. Finally, Gerard mentioned that there were more Hessian deserters in the area, but patrols of natives and French militia had recaptured many of them.[249]

Two days later, Benjamin Whitcomb's squad returned with two prisoners from the Twenty-Ninth Regiment of Foot.[250] The captives were not particularly talkative but confirmed that large numbers of sailing ships were about to move south. Arnold still had his third team of scouts collecting information but wondered if Gerard had compromised the secret missions. Ominously, the weather was bad, with frequent cold rains.

On September 19, Arnold feared the enemy had extended its grip around him again, as with Windmill Point two weeks earlier. Still anchored south of Isle La Motte and waiting for the eventual confrontation with the British fleet, he ordered the *Liberty* north and east. The maneuver wasn't too risky. Alburgh was a mile distant, allowing plenty of room to maneuver. Arnold continued to seek as much intelligence as possible, and he needed to keep tabs on the eastern portion of the lake. For all the colonials knew, the enemy might attempt to portage smaller gunboats and bateaux into Missisquoi Bay.

It didn't take long for Arnold to encounter the enemy. After sailing into the channel, a Frenchman appeared on the Isle La Motte coast. He swung his arms and shouted in his native tongue, motioning for the Americans to come and pick him up. The captain of the *Liberty* released a bateau to do so, but the

Arnold ordered the *Liberty* to sail between Isle La Motte and Alburgh to look for signs of the enemy. *Photo by Armand Messier and Northern Vermont Aerial Photography.*

As the *Liberty* scouted off the coast of Isle La Motte, it discovered dozens of hidden enemy canoes. *Photo by Armand Messier and Northern Vermont Aerial Photography.*

crew was cautious. They slowed their approach and ordered the Frenchman on shore to swim to them. Suspecting a trap, the *Liberty* repositioned itself, guns pointing at the tree line. Unable to attract the Americans any closer, the Frenchman went back up the beach. Chaos erupted. Hundreds of natives, French Canadian militia and regulars emerged from the woods and unleashed a musket volley.[251] Three Americans on the bateau were wounded before the tiny craft responded with its swivel guns. The *Liberty* fired a broadside, and the enemy retreated into the forest. The wounded men eventually died of their wounds. The bateau returned to the *Liberty*, and the ship continued its patrol. They spied several dozen birch-bark canoes tucked against Isle La Motte's eastern shore.[252] The implications were clear. As long as the American fleet was in the narrow reaches of the lake, the British land forces were going to try to leapfrog them and harass their flanks. Enemy forces had been operating on Alburgh for days. Now they were swarming over Isle La Motte.

During the final days of summer, the British significantly upgraded their presence on Île aux Noix. Beyond the blockhouses and the improved earthworks, a battery of twelve-pound cannons and several howitzers were placed on the island. Increasing numbers of soldiers used it as a layover point as the British grip on the Lake Champlain islands tightened. Île aux Noix, just a few miles from Missisquoi Bay, was now a substantial military position.[253]

Chapter 6

"THEY WERE RIGHT HERE"

Fall of 1776

On September 23, the American fleet sailed south once again, looking for a spot to conceal itself, assess the situation and prepare for the approach of the enemy. It traveled between Grand Isle and Cumberland Head and kept a watchful eye on the location of the exchange of fire from early September. Arnold brought the fleet to rest around Valcour Island, on the west side of the lake, just south of present-day Plattsburgh. He knew it would be difficult for the larger British ships to maneuver there.[254] The chaotic colors of the seasonal foliage provided a bit of foreshadowing. The fiery reds, yellows and oranges started to dominate the trees and the shorelines. The *Liberty* was dispatched to collect supplies for the fleet.[255]

While the repositioning of ships was unfolding on the lake, another enemy deserter showed up at Bayley's camp on the Connecticut River.[256]

On September 28, Arnold wrote to his superiors at Ticonderoga and Crown Point. He disclosed information from his scouts that the British were all over the northern reaches. Alburgh, Isle La Motte, North Hero and Metcalf's settlement in Missisquoi Bay were all occupied or being watched by the enemy. Additionally, it was apparent that they were putting in considerable effort trying to catch deserters from British, Hessian or Tory units.[257]

By September 30, natives aligned with the Crown had raided as far south as the Onion River. Three people were taken prisoner and were likely on their way to a Quebec prison.[258] Another recently completed vessel, the *Trumbull*, joined the American fleet that day.

On October 1, Arnold received more valuable intelligence. Stiles had safely returned.[259] Some details conflicted with those given by Gerard just a few days prior. The British wanted to draw the American fleet back north, to get the rebels within range of the recently constructed cannon embankments along the lakeshore. There were substantial British forces at the Lacolle River, just north of the forty-fifth parallel. Stiles reported that there were hundreds of natives in the woods around Windmill Point.[260] Arnold wrote to General Gates and suggested that 1,500 American soldiers sail north. He believed it would take that number of men to challenge the enemy and wrest control of Isle La Motte. The weather continued to be cold and rainy, with gusts of wind ripping leaves from the trees.

The British fleet was ready, and the hunt began on October 3. They were prepared to initiate a cold-weather campaign. Their ships left St. Jean and Île aux Noix and arrived near Windmill Point.[261] The smaller craft pushed south first; the larger ships still navigated the Richelieu. They looked for their prey. They wanted to destroy the American fleet. Anchored miles to the south, behind Valcour Island, it was nowhere to be found.

Meanwhile, on land, the colonials still tried to shore up their defenses in the New Hampshire Grants. It wasn't going well. Major Butler was dispatched

The British invasion fleet sailed near the Alburgh coast prior to the Battle of Valcour Island. *Photo by Armand Messier and Northern Vermont Aerial Photography.*

with a fresh unit to the Onion River garrison. He had orders to arrest any of the nearly eighty men unsatisfactorily performing their duties. By October 5, fresh soldiers manned the posts along the river. The disillusioned men were placed under guard at Mount Independence.[262]

On October 6, the American fleet got more reinforcements. The galley *Washington* arrived. Just a few miles away, the British force moved south past Point au Fer. They left four companies at the base, which the Americans had recently abandoned, probably because it was too far north to defend.[263] Four days later, on October 10, the British moved farther onto Lake Champlain. The arrival of the *Inflexible*, one of their flotilla's largest and most powerful vessels, significantly increased the firepower of their force.[264] As they wondered where Arnold's fleet lurked, they spent the night anchored south of Isle La Motte, near North Hero and Grand Isle.[265]

The battle that followed five days later has been recognized as one of the most significant military engagements in American history. Arnold's navy hid behind Valcour Island as the much larger and superior British force moved south on October 11. Arnold had chosen the area carefully, knowing that it would be nearly impossible for the enemy to come against his ships all at once. He had studied the depth of the lake and the wind directions and understood the capabilities of sailing vessels. Most of the British force had sailed beyond Valcour before Arnold sent the *Royal Savage* out to get their attention. Both sides experienced difficulties at this early stage. Fighting a north wind, many of the British forces were unable to maneuver into position. What frustrated them affected the *Royal Savage* as well, as it ran aground on Valcour attempting to make it back to the rebel line.

The *Royal Savage* was taken out of action. The American fleet was suddenly down one of its larger vessels, and the real fighting was yet to begin. The larger British ships slowly moved into Valcour Bay. Arnold's remaining ships opened fire on the approaching enemy. For the rest of the morning, volleys were exchanged. Savage fire raked the approaching British ships, as they had difficulty getting into position. The fighting lasted throughout the afternoon and into the evening. One of the British gunboats was hit. Some of its ammunition exploded, and the vessel sank. Arnold's fleet suffered another loss when the *Philadelphia* took on too much water. It sank to the bottom of Valcour Bay as the fighting subsided at dark.

Nightfall was the chance for Arnold, the ultimate survivor, to help his fleet escape. His crews muffled their oars as much as possible, dimmed onboard lights and squeezed between the enemy ships and New York's western shore. By morning, he had put considerable distance between the two fleets.

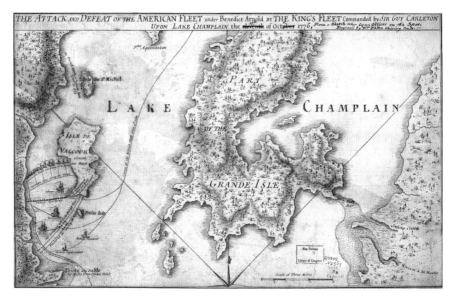

The British fleet engaged Arnold's ships at the Battle of Valcour Island. *Courtesy of the Library of Congress.*

However, most of the British ships were in far better condition than the American vessels. The British pursued, caught up with and engaged the Americans again on October 12. A running cannonade unfolded for several hours. Slowly, damaged American vessels fell away from the line, including the *Spitfire*, which sank to the bottom of Lake Champlain.

Arnold ordered the remaining American ships to flee south into what is known as Arnold's Bay near the present-day towns of Panton and Vergennes. He burned the rest of his fleet. The British had won a major victory, but at an exceptional cost. Arnold's ability to construct enough ships that stood in the way of the mighty British navy cost the forces of the Crown dearly. If the present offensive was not successful, they would be delayed an entire fighting season.

With the weather getting colder, the British had a decision to make. They could press their advantage and move against Ticonderoga. Or they could assess the situation, analyze the American defenses and return the next spring with an even larger fighting force. After dispatching Arnold and the American navy, Guy Carleton pushed south, prepared to see what else the colonials might throw in his way.

During the third week of October, portions of Carleton's fleet patrolled the lake north of Ticonderoga. Bands of Tories, including one group of several dozen led by Justus Sherwood, joined the British army near Crown Point.[266] They probed the American defenses but decided to wait. As the Americans had painfully learned a year earlier, northeastern winters did not aid an attacking army. Carleton ordered his ships to sail back to Quebec.

With the British in control of northern Lake Champlain, they fortified their positions at Île aux Noix and St. Jean. Their vessels returned to the Richelieu River, and their soldiers remained at the Point au Fer White House.[267] Work was immediately undertaken to make the small fortress a viable forward post throughout the winter.

During the first week of November, elements of William Digby's unit were at Point au Fer. They found the floating body of one of their artillerymen, who drowned on October 13. They recovered the corpse and buried him at an unrecorded location. A few ships were still at Point au Fer on November 6. A heavy fog set in, and General Simon Frazer ordered the vessels to move a short distance south and east. A group of British infantrymen spent the night on Isle La Motte.[268]

In the final days of November, a colonial bateau departed from farmland on the banks of the Onion River. Settlers had harvested their potatoes and Indian corn. It was a supply run to Fort Ticonderoga and Mount Independence. The craft managed to go unmolested by the British and their raiding parties. On December 3, as it approached the fortifications, lookouts

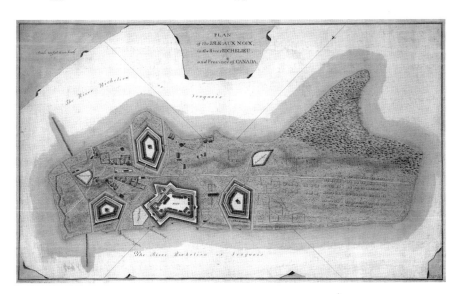

As winter set in, the British planned to make substantial upgrades to Île aux Noix. The base was only miles from Missisquoi Bay. *Courtesy of the Library of Congress.*

mistook it for an enemy ship.[269] After a few tense moments, the situation was resolved. Based on the supply problem the army experienced during the previous three seasons, the food was welcome.

The war was now a year and a half old. Schemes and plots were hatched. More scout missions were unleashed throughout the winter. Jacob Bayley, from his base in the upper Connecticut River, waited to hear back from the natives at St. Francis. Perhaps aware that relations with certain native bands could be negotiated, Bayley was attempting to drive a wedge between the English government and its native allies.[270] In war, any advantage is worth pursuing.

Chapter 7

"WHAT COMES NEXT?"

Winter and Spring of 1777

W inters in the Northeast are unforgiving. The twenty or so British soldiers stationed opposite Isle La Motte, on Point au Fer, experienced raw and brutal cold. The same conditions hindered the men stationed at St. Jean and Île aux Noix. Aside from staying alive, their goal was to look south along Lake Champlain. If the Americans returned to northern regions, the vantage point from Point au Fer would give the British plenty of advance warning.[271]

The colonials were doing no such thing. In the fall, after the British were victorious at Valcour Island, the Americans had galvanized a significant defense of the Champlain Valley. By the final weeks of October, there were thousands of colonial soldiers at Fort Ticonderoga and Mount Independence. Those numbers, and the approach of winter, had been enough to return the British to Quebec.

With the immediate threat to the Champlain Valley removed, most of the colonial soldiers were sent south to areas where they could make a difference. Many of them saw plenty of action at places that have been etched into the history books. After a series of defeats around New York City and Long Island, Washington crossed the Delaware River, and the Battle of Trenton was fought on December 26. It was a surprising victory for the rebels.

Meanwhile, the British planned their next moves in the Champlain Valley, and local geography would play a major factor. General Johnny Burgoyne was about to return from England with a substantial fighting force. His plan was to take Fort Ticonderoga, march through Upstate New York and divide

New England from the rest of the colonies. It was ambitious, and it could work if executed appropriately.

By late March, at least some of the waters of the Richelieu River were free of ice, and the British moved two warships closer to Point au Fer. The open waters provided easier opportunities to resupply the garrison.[272] It was the first step in reasserting their dominance.

By April 13, most of their navy was on the lake. The larger vessels were used as support ships. The smaller bateaux traveled south with natives and regulars. Benjamin Whitcomb reported that the enemy operated around Cumberland Head, near present-day Plattsburgh, across from the Lake Champlain islands. Shots were exchanged between small war parties. It foreshadowed events to come.[273]

In May, tensions between Yorkers and Green Mountain Boys, on the one side, and patriots and Tories on the other, played out in different ways. Sympathetic groups moved north to join General Burgoyne in Quebec as he organized his invasion plans. A group of thirteen Tories traveled through Pittsford, led by Benjamin Cole. Twenty-two local militiamen caught up with them in the town of Monkton. The Tories were captured, tried and held at Fort Ticonderoga.[274] On May 13, they were interrogated and admitted to trying to join the British army.[275]

By late May, the continentals had heard more from their scouts. The Americans knew the British were coming—it was just a matter of when and with how much force. In this case, two large British vessels, seven gunboats and nearly forty bateaux operated west and south of the Onion River near present-day Burlington.[276] These were not isolated movements. Simon Fraser, the head of Burgoyne's light infantry, sailed past Windmill Point in early June and was at Point au Fer, preparing for the movement of the entire British army.[277]

On June 13, the British invasion force again moved south. This was different than in the fall of 1776. The Americans had little or no fleet. The British had two ships that brandished twenty or more cannons. The *Royal George* had twenty-four, and the *Inflexible* had twenty. The rest of the fleet was well armed. The schooner *Maria* had fourteen. *Carlton* had another dozen. The radeau *Thunderer* brandished eighteen. There were two dozen gunboats. To add insult to injury, the British had captured, repaired and improved several vessels from Arnold's shattered fleet. *Washington* now had sixteen cannons; the cutter *Lee* had ten. The *Jersey* threatened with seven.[278] This force was more than a match for anything that remained of the American navy. The rebels had so few ships that another large battle wasn't even a

In June 1777, the British returned to Lake Champlain. Their objective was to retake Fort Ticonderoga. The fleet sailed west of Alburgh on its way south. *Photo by Armand Messier and Northern Vermont Aerial Photography.*

possibility. The English had such an advantage that the larger vessels were considered escorts for the scores of bateaux carrying infantry. Burgoyne made sure his flanks were protected. When his flotilla sailed, there were twelve cannons stationed at Point au Fer.[279] Lieutenant William Twiss of the army corps of engineers was tasked with upgrades to the peninsula, and a group from the Twenty-Fourth Regiment guarded the engineers.

Every army requires a solid supply chain to sustain itself, and Burgoyne's was no different. Control of Lake Champlain allowed free movement of replacements and reinforcements. When the invasion commenced, he gave his army orders to confiscate supplies from locals. The Twenty-Ninth Regiment of Foot was assigned to guard the critical fort of St. Jean. The units packed on board the naval vessels and bateaux were the Ninth, Twentieth, Twenty-First, Twenty-Fourth, Thirty-First, Forty-Seventh, Fifty-Third and Sixty-Second Regiments of the English army. The Hessian regiments moved with them.

On June 16, Burgoyne's invasion force pushed south. It left the recently finished fortifications at Île aux Noix behind, now sparsely occupied by men of the Twentieth Regiment of Foot. The next day, most of the fleet was between Point au Fer and Cumberland Head. The Hessian units crossed

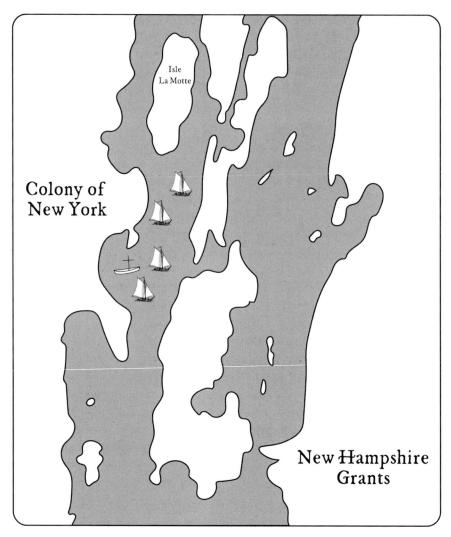

On the way to retake Fort Ticonderoga, the British fleet sailed by the Lake Champlain islands. *Artwork by Lindsay DiDio.*

the lake and camped on Isle La Motte for the evening. Ironically, another vessel used by the British had been constructed by the Americans in the first days of the Revolution, in 1775. Renamed *Loyal Convert*, it was paradoxically being used to put down the rebellion.[280]

The fleet moved over the broad lake and approached where Champlain narrows considerably, near the present-day towns Shelburne and Charlotte, where small bands were released on the shores to make sure passage was safe.

By June 23, the British fleet was at the mouth of Otter Creek.[281] An American scout returned to Fort Ticonderoga and Mount Independence carrying the grim news. The powerful British army and navy were now within striking distance of reconquering the Champlain Valley.

Chapter 8

"UNDER THE BOOT OF THE CROWN"

Summer and Fall of 1777

In early July, nearly 250 natives rowed canoes into Otter Creek, near present-day Ferrisburgh. Small bands scoured each bank, pointing muskets at the tree line, protecting the war canoes as they moved upriver. They provided support for the British boats descending on Ticonderoga and Mount Independence. They cleared locals and suspected rebels, took prisoners and pushed farther inward. Near present-day Salisbury, the Graves, Weeks and Parker families were all displaced.[282]

On the evening of July 5, American general Arthur St. Clair judged that he was not going to be able to hold the Lake Champlain forts. The British had already outmaneuvered the colonial defenses by placing cannons on the hills to the southwest. Ticonderoga was totally exposed. The enemy controlled the lake, and he had only one-quarter the number of the Crown's soldiers. Coming south were ten thousand men. He had barely three thousand colonials. St. Clair ordered both Fort Ticonderoga and Mount Independence abandoned, thinking it was better to live and fight another day.

Under the cover of darkness, the Americans left their defenses behind. One night later, most of the army had retreated toward Castleton and Rutland. Some units under Seth Warner stopped to catch their breath. On the morning of July 7, the Battle of Hubbardton erupted as British and Hessian soldiers attacked Warner's forces. This was the only large battle fought on Vermont soil. During the fighting, the Indian and Tory scouting parties rejoined the British forces. After the American retreat, local families were further harassed. In some cases, their property was burned.[283]

The British retook Fort Ticonderoga in July 1777. *Photograph by the author.*

Surprisingly, in the midst of a military defeat, Vermont effectively declared its independence from the British, and from the colonies of New York and New Hampshire. At the Windsor Convention on July 8 and then again at Manchester on July 11, Vermont leaders adopted a new constitution. During these meetings, the Allen family and others laid the legal groundwork for identifying land owned by Loyalists. Vermont's new government was interested in confiscating those plots.[284] It feared a groundswell of support from those who favored the Crown and knew of groups organizing to support the enemy.[285] In other cases, rebel families relocated to places like Havervill and Newbury to get far away from the British.

Despite the recent defeat in the West, the mechanics of the war machine did not stop in Newbury. Officers from the Northeast Kingdom still worked on building the route between the Connecticut River and St. Jean. One discussion involved command officers and Captain Thomas Johnson sending Solomon Stephens to inform Metcalf on the up-to-date road scheme.[286] It is logical to assume the Americans were not totally aware of Metcalf's misfortune at this point.

In the central area of the Green Mountains, militia units started construction on Fort Mott, where Otter Creek runs through Pittsford. It had hemlock walls and covered about three-quarters of an acre. A blockhouse-type building was at the center. It was almost exclusively for defensive purposes. With the entire British army now camped near Lake George and Skenesborough, and with constant war parties on the move, locals wanted a rally point.

Appropriate historical attention has been devoted to the Saratoga campaign. Burgoyne followed the desperate American army through Upstate New York. With each passing day, he stretched his supply lines. He sent a detachment to Bennington, hoping to rally Loyalist sympathies and seize colonial supplies stored there. The detachment never reached its objective and was instead defeated about ten miles west of Bennington, in Walloomsic, New York, on August 16. Many Green Mountain Boys participated in this engagement, known as the Battle of Bennington. The main British force moved south and west in pursuit of General Gates and the colonial army. Aspects of that campaign had a local impact in Vermont not usually explored by historians.

By September 26, Burgoyne's supply lines were stretched very thin. Originally, he had planned for forces in southern New York to link with his army. They never did, and soon his men were up against the colonial army and countless locals throughout the countryside. Burgoyne didn't have the appropriate amount of food to feed an army in hostile territory. The Hessian soldiers stationed at Mount Independence suffered nearly as much as the British soldiers approaching Saratoga. They were eating rations of wheat bread, water and salt pork. When a bateau arrived from Canada full of potatoes, it was a welcome addition to the menu.[287] Just weeks later, in early October, the British army surrendered at Saratoga. The forces that hadn't been defeated were left to retreat north through the Champlain Valley.

In November, British-allied natives targeted central Vermont. About 150 were on the prowl in Pittsford but decided against a full attack on the now nearly complete Fort Mott. However, they harassed and killed locals.[288]

Meanwhile, the settlement in Prattsburgh, present-day Swanton, suffered from the opportunism of war. Metcalf was still detained in Quebec. His property was in the care of Jessie Weldon, the first inhabitant of what would become St. Albans. Weldon had been employed by Metcalf and looked over the estate. He couldn't prevent others from taking advantage of Metcalf's misfortune. Two men, William Hay and a Mr. Brady, descended on the Missisquoi settlement and stole cattle and farm animals. The animals were brought to butchers in Quebec.[289]

As winter approached, Frye Bayley, who had first scouted the northern road route, embarked on another mission. It was a prisoner exchange. The American leadership agreed to return a British lieutenant Singleton in exchange for an American prisoner in Quebec. Bayley and a few other patriots were intimately aware of the paths through the frontier. They

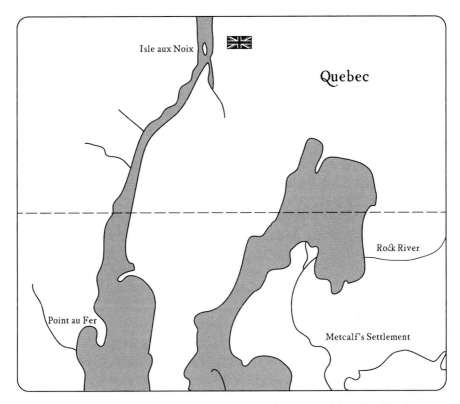

As the Saratoga campaign developed in Upstate New York, Simon Metcalf suffered more misfortune. *Artwork by Lindsay DiDio.*

departed from the northern reaches of the Connecticut River with their prisoner on December 10. When the excursion arrived on the banks of the Missisquoi River two hours after sunset on the evening of December 15, not many people were around. The settlement was just getting by. The first snows of winter were on the ground. Metcalf and his family were gone, still being held in Quebec. The settlement wasn't abandoned, but the locals were in rough shape. Bayley went to Metcalf's log cabin and found two nearly starving Abenakis inside, cooking in the kitchen area. The natives shared their meager portions of porridge.

The next morning, the small group waited as two men repaired their snowshoes. Frye Bayley cooked up some cornmeal into cakes for the rest of the journey north. They proceeded along the meandering path of the Missisquoi River and saw thin patches of ice covering the shallow, slow-moving water north of the falls. They crossed Missisquoi Bay in a boat obtained from the settlement. It was dark and cloudy, so they

As the British retreated north on Lake Champlain after the Battle of Saratoga, they sailed beyond Isle La Motte. *Photo by Armand Messier and Northern Vermont Aerial Photography.*

When the defeated British left the Champlain Valley, their boats sailed around Windmill Point in Alburgh. *Photo by Armand Messier and Northern Vermont Aerial Photography.*

were unable to rely on the stars and camped farther north than they wanted to. Bayley gathered water with his hat and shared his cornmeal cakes with his travelers. At dawn, they set out for the South River, which emerges close to Île aux Noix.[290] Bayley spent considerable time in Quebec completing the prisoner exchange. He returned to the colonies through a different area.

Chapter 9

"THE ENEMY TO THE NORTH"

1778

While the main events of the Revolutionary War shifted farther south, plenty of smaller but significant events unfolded in the Champlain Valley. As George Washington huddled with his army at Valley Forge, British forces were still in Quebec. With a substantial enemy force that close, sustained conflict in northern Vermont was inevitable.

In 1778, new British leadership made the overall decision to strengthen the defenses along the forty-fifth parallel. Some work had already been done at Île aux Noix, but it received more attention. An entirely new fort was planned.[291] The existing structures served as a starting point, and engineers were told to prepare new defensive emplacements.[292] William Twiss, head of Frederick Haldimand's corps of engineers, drew up plans for the defensive measures.[293] There would be a blockhouse constructed on the Lake Champlain islands and further improvements to Point au Fer.

War does not always wait for warm weather, and in late February, the British decided to take action south of the border. Colonials had stored some of their wheat harvest in the Moses Pierson blockhouse in Shelburne. It was in the southwestern area of town, near the lakeshore, opposite tiny Meach Island. British spies had learned that Thomas Chittenden wanted sleighs to transport much of the wheat to rebel positions in Rutland and Castleton. Colonial militia departed Fort Vengeance in Pittsford, arrived in Shelburne and started to thresh the grain. Local lore has it that a Tory, perhaps Philo Emmery, went north and shared the information. The British normally did not operate in the dead of winter but saw an opportunity to disrupt colonial supply efforts.

On or around the morning of March 9, approximately fifty-seven soldiers of the Eighty-Fourth Regiment of British Loyalists trekked from Île aux Noix to present-day Alburgh. They donned their skates, pulled supplies in sleds and hugged the western shores of the Lake Champlain islands. Some of these men may have been drinking heavily before the mission. Robert McKinnon was the officer in charge. They embarked dressed as Native Americans and probably stopped at Point au Fer.[294] As they traveled, they camped on the islands each night and used isolated hamlets to avoid detection. The colonials were lucky and observed their approach. At 6:00 a.m. on March 12, the unit tried to launch a surprise attack.[295] The engagement did not go well for the raiders.

About twenty locals and colonial militia were present when the raid began. The attackers came in from the east and followed a small stream to their objective. The sounds of gunshots echoed through snow-covered woods. The colonials were behind the relative safety of the blockhouse walls. The attackers managed to set the structure on fire twice, but the defenders extinguished the flames. Soon, six Tories were dead. Another dozen were wounded and five were captured. As they retreated, blood flowed freely onto the ice-covered creek, causing it to turn red. During the retreat to Quebec, several more of the attackers perished. The raid had been a disaster for the attackers. Their retreat was so grim that when wounded soldiers died, their bodies were stuffed into ice cracks on Lake Champlain. Only three or four colonials lost their lives during the engagement.

A crisis of a different sort hit the young republic in March. The towns between the Connecticut River and Lake Champlain, attempting to organize an individual government separate from existing colonies, were victims of their own success. Sixteen towns from western New Hampshire attempted to politically join Vermont. Initially, the idea was not opposed by the young Vermont government. New Hampshire, which had reacted much differently than New York with respect to Vermont's independence, was not particularly pleased.[296]

At about the same time, Roger Stevens, his family and a group of twenty-three Loyalists arrived in the area of St. Jean. They no longer wanted to be surrounded by rebels. Prior to the outbreak of hostilities, Stevens had a hand in developing mills along Otter Creek in Pittsford. Their route to Quebec took him through northern Vermont. He quickly developed a relationship with British major Christopher Carleton, who had designs on returning and wreaking havoc on colonials in the Champlain Valley.[297]

Even though the British had been defeated at Saratoga, the war had not departed the Champlain Valley. On April 26, Schuyler wrote to George

Washington that half a dozen of the enemy's largest ships were back on the lake, sailing as far south as Fort Ticonderoga.[298] With their return to the lake, British installations appear to have been relatively unmolested. In May, one report indicated the men stationed at Point au Fer believed the closest enemy presence was over twelve miles away.[299]

In June, Haldimand formally took over Guy Carleton's position as the governor of Quebec. Much of the British army had been redeployed elsewhere, but he still had military resources to call on. His primary goal was to keep colonials from invading Quebec again. He ordered the navy to constantly patrol the lake, and he made sure there was a constant British presence south of the forty-fifth parallel.

Colonials in central regions of the Green Mountains sensed this, and during the summer of 1778, they moved to shore up their own defenses. They began work on Fort Ranger, built on Otter Creek in Rutland. This base covered two full acres, had a two-story blockhouse and was constructed to host a permanent garrison.[300]

In June, thirteen English vessels carried nearly five hundred soldiers to Crown Point. They operated as an advanced scouting party.[301] The British sailed up and down the lake at will. There were still significant numbers of troops at Île au Noix, and St. Jean, and there were nearly sixty stationed at Point au Fer. By the end of the month, eight warships still operated around the Lake Champlain islands. Additionally, their gunboats still patrolled Vermont's coastlines.[302]

To the east, the engineering aspects of the military road still had life. Moses Hazen, whom Benedict Arnold met in 1775 during the Quebec invasion, now worked on broadening the Bayley project. British authorities became concerned about another invasion. The area where Hazen had chosen to work was problematic for the English. If he selected a westward route, it would connect to Missisquoi Bay or the Richelieu River. If Hazen took the project north, it would cross the eastern portions of the Missisquoi River and provide access to the Yamaska River, in the heart of Quebec. Hazen could even veer farther east and connect with Lake Memphremagog. Such a path posed less of a threat to greater Quebec, but memories of Arnold in Maine were not that distant.[303] The colonial force had already trekked through impossible terrain once to invade Quebec. It might happen again.

In August, Governor Haldimand ordered his first raid. The force was commanded by John Peters, and it attacked settlements along the Onion River. During the mission, a few homesteads and mills were attacked, but it didn't go as well as planned.[304]

Back in Quebec, Simon Metcalf worked to clear his name and reclaim his land. On August 29, while still being held, he wrote to British authorities. He had spent almost two years away from his settlement, pleading with authorities to let him return to Missisquoi. Metcalf claimed that his house and properties had been destroyed.[305]

Meanwhile, the war continued. Elements of the Twenty-Ninth Regiment of Foot, which had been regulated to support activities for the Burgoyne invasion in 1777, returned to St. Jean in early September. By the twelfth, the 120 men had been assigned to the fortifications at Île aux Noix, just a stone's throw from Windmill Point, Isle La Motte and Missisquoi Bay.[306] The arrival of these troops to the area foreshadowed the return of future hostilities.

In October, the fledgling Vermont government temporarily smoothed things over with New Hampshire. The sixteen border towns along the Connecticut River still waited to see if they could officially become part of Vermont. To maintain support for overall independence, the Vermont legislature voted to deny the wayward communities.[307] The issue was not dead, however.

Considerable British resources were brought together just north of Lake Champlain in late September and early October. Ninety-six men from the Thirty-First Regiment were transferred to Île aux Noix, and they camped on the northern edge of the island. Fifty men from the Fifty-Third Regiment soon joined them. Some, men from the Twenty-Ninth Regiment, were also given orders to prepare for operations to the south.[308] Another thirty men came from Sir Johnson's force. British leadership asked for help from their Caughnawaga allies, and approximately eighty warriors arrived and camped south of the island.[309] By the middle of October, the strike force was prepared.[310]

History remembers it as Carleton's Raid.

The raiders were carried in the large vessels and bateaux. The larger ships *Maria* and *Carleton* were the main escorts. During the first day, the force made a little more than twelve miles. They stopped at Point au Fer; by nightfall, the entire force was camped on the northern edge of Isle La Motte.[311] On the night of October 25, the redcoats made another twelve miles and anchored on the west side of the lake, near the mouth of the Ausable River. Colin Campbell, a local, visited and tried to provide useful information. They kept a watchful eye to the east, suspecting the Green Mountains were infested with rebels.[312]

The third and final day of travel was on October 26. They moved through morning fog, sailed another dozen miles and anchored off Flat Rock Point, near Willsboro, New York, across from Shelburne, Vermont.[313] They waited

Native groups allied with the British supported their raids into the Green Mountains. *Artwork by Josh Sinz.*

nearly five days as their soldiers scouted the woods. On October 30, they hugged the New York shore and made it to Split Rock, directly across from the mouth of Otter Creek.[314]

In the first days of November, small parties of Green Mountain Boys organized, aware of the threat on the lake. Bands of rebels in bateaux hugged the eastern shore and tried to assess the strength of the enemy force. On November 5, eighty British and allied natives landed around Chimney Point, looking for rebels.[315] Roger Stevens, whom the colonials had harassed and imprisoned earlier in the war, was a part of this group. Stevens still had family in Pittsford but was ordered by bis British commanders to have no contact with his brother. As they went farther ashore, prisoners were taken and boated to the *Maria*.[316] A stronger force was sent into the woods around Otter Creek the next day. They had orders to destroy the local sawmill. The New Haven blockhouse, constructed before the war to ward off Yorkers, was probably burned at this time.[317] Enacting something of a scorched-earth policy, they burned multiple homes and confiscated hidden supplies found in barns. By November 7, they were on the outskirts of Middlebury.[318] They searched the countryside for hours, burning more homes and a few barns. Many of the inhabitants fled in front of the British advance. On November 8, they zigzagged across Otter Creek, again setting the torch to multiple buildings. The next day, the force was back in the Vergennes and camped along the lower falls.[319] More homes were destroyed, and farm animals were confiscated.

By this time, the enemy had been on land for several days and was worried that rebel forces might organize. A few more limited, quick incursions were approved. The navy's vessels were anchored at the mouth of Otter Creek and could send in bateaux full of regulars if reinforcements were needed. Carleton wanted to observe the operation firsthand and arrived in Vergennes on November 9. A small raiding party was sent to the town of Monkton.[320] With the strike complete, the British fell back to the mouth of Otter Creek. Numerous cattle and more prisoners were loaded onto the *Maria* and *Carleton*. The mop-up activities lasted another day. As they departed for points north, they sailed along the eastern shore and burned three more homes. These were likely in the town of Charlotte.[321] Local lore in St. Albans suggests that the first settlers in St. Albans Bay, including Jesse Weldon, were taken prisoner and brought to Quebec at some point.[322] This may have happened during the final acts of Carleton's Raid.

The raiding force made it to Grand Isle. The fleet anchored in a small bay near one of the tiny islands on the north side of the island.[323] The next day and evening, the flotilla battled foul weather and got only as far as Point au Fer.

By November 12, the incursion force was back at Île aux Noix. As winter approached, most of the Twenty-Ninth Regiment of Foot was deployed on the island. The days were shorter and became much colder.

Chapter 10

"THE WAR CONTINUES"

1779

When January arrived, the British Twenty-Ninth Regiment of Foot was still on Île aux Noix.[324] They passed the short, cold, dark days of winter knowing that a rebel assault was unlikely.

On February 9, British officers went to the Abenaki village of St. Francis in Quebec. Rumors had spread that the Americans might try a cold-weather assault. Local natives heard stories that the American military had prepared large numbers of snowshoes for a possible invasion through Missisquoi Bay.[325]

Meanwhile, Simon Metcalf was still in Quebec. Days after British officials met with their native allies, he appeared before Judge Southouse and provided a list of everything destroyed on his property.[326] He asked about a release date but was not given an answer. Metcalf wondered if the judge had been influenced by private interests who had their own designs on his lands at Missisquoi.

That winter, the young Vermont Republic struggled with how to protect its citizens. The new General Assembly met, and a "Board of War" was formed. It knew that southern regions were easier to protect than the north. The board established a line of defense that stretched from Castleton to Pittsford. Anyone who lived above that line, which encompassed more than half of the young republic, was urged to move.[327] The legislature formally acknowledged that the sixteen New Hampshire towns along the Connecticut River were under the jurisdiction of the older colony.[328] However, as the Republic of Vermont asserted its independence, that issue was still not entirely resolved.

In March, General Schuyler wrote to Washington about striking around St. Jean. He wanted to burn the British ships that would emerge onto the lake in the spring. Despite floating the idea, Schuyler cautioned about the deployment of resources in Missisquoi Bay. He feared British scouts were constantly in the area.[329] The plans for the attack were not entirely shelved, however. On March 6, Washington wrote to Moses Hazen and ordered him to continue the roadwork Metcalf and Jacob Bayley had initiated almost three years earlier.[330]

By the time the ice melted, enemy ships again sailed the lake. Like Arnold in 1776, the British were concerned about the shallowness of some areas. The commander of their fleet, William Chambers, prepared a manual with maps that detailed navigational hazards. Captains were urged to steer clear of the water on the northern edge of Isle La Motte due to its shallowness and the danger of reef rocks.[331]

In the eastern Green Mountains, work recommenced on the Bayley-Hazen Road. A segment stretched through northern Peacham and into Cabot, and another blockhouse was built to protect the workers and serve as a defensive location. This location was chosen for its line of sight, as it was the highest point in town.[332]

The incursions from Quebec weighed on colonial efforts to protect southern towns. The colonials decided that Fort Mott in Pittsford and Fort Ranger in Rutland were not enough, and another stockade garrison was constructed in Castleton. This one was dubbed Fort Warren and was built in about a month and a half, between early April and mid-May.[333] The settlers around Fort Mott received intelligence that British soldiers, Loyalists and natives were on the lake, approaching the southern regions. Colonial militia scouted in present-day Basin Harbor and were ambushed by a party of Indians. At least one colonial was killed, and the others were captured and taken back to the British ships.[334]

After four years of war in the Champlain Valley, Loyalists saw the writing on the wall. Those who owned property in the colonies and made the mistake of supporting the king, were not going to be able to return to their lives. Many of them fled north to Quebec. This was the case on May 18, when British ships picked up seventeen Loyalists on Ise La Motte.[335] They left everything they had known behind.

Meanwhile, the British feared the Americans had increased their strength on the upper Connecticut River. Reports surfaced that Benjamin Whitcomb had been ordered there with about six hundred men. They feared that behind Whitcomb were another one thousand American

soldiers coming up the Connecticut.[336] By their information, he planned to march west to the Missisquoi River and was part of a larger invasion. Officers at Île aux Noix ordered scouts to Missisquoi Bay on June 2.[337] British command wanted to ensure that the preparatory work hadn't started, virtually under their noses, with Missisquoi Bay so nearby. The scouts were on the bay and probed the Missisquoi River and woods of present-day Swanton and Highgate for three days. More British scouts were in the bay around June 7.[338]

About two weeks later, on June 20, another mission went to Missisquoi Bay and yielded results.[339] British ensign Battersby and his men captured three individuals traveling through the area. The interrogators had difficulty determining if they were American deserters or scouts. They were sent to

Opposite: The British ship *Maria* operated on Lake Champlain throughout the summer and fall of 1779. *Artwork by Josh Sinz.*

Above: British gunboats sailed unmolested on Lake Champlain in support of their raiding parties. *Artwork by Josh Sinz.*

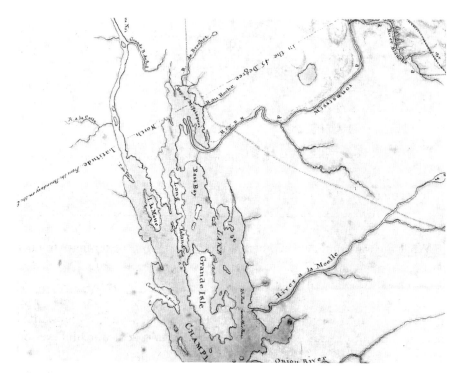

When the British became concerned about the military road through the Green Mountains, they sent out scouts to evaluate the enemy work. *Courtesy of the Library of Congress.*

Chambly and further questioned. The British did learn that the work on the Hazen-Bayley military road continued.

Dozens of miles away, laborers felled trees, cleared stumps and set the road. American forces in the region were primarily for defense. Another blockhouse was built. This one was in Walden and furthered the defensive line of support that was expanding through the Green Mountains.[340] A final blockhouse was built in Greensboro, directly west of Caspian Lake.

On Lake Champlain, Ebenezer Allen was one of the first settlers to move to South Hero. Despite the constant raids, scouting missions and hostilities, he built a log cabin in the thick woods.[341]

In late July, Catherine Metcalf sent a letter to the Quebec authorities, asking that her husband be set free. She tried to convince the magistrate that his release would allow him to work to pay off his creditors and support his children.[342]

By September, the road through the northern Green Mountains had progressed nearly fifty-four miles. Its course had shifted farther east than

Simon Metcalf's first plans. Originally, he had wanted it to proceed into the Missisquoi Bay area. Now, Hazen had constructed it up to Westfield, just south of Montgomery, at present-day Hazen's Notch.[343]

That same month, British commanders decided to rely more heavily on Loyalist forces. Robert Rogers, who came to fame with his exploits during the French and Indian War, was asked to organize regiments of Loyalists. Roger Stevens, who had participated in the prior fall's raids, was named recruiting officer.[344] These units, while organized in Quebec, would operate on Lake Champlain.

By September 30, the British had good intelligence that related to Moses Hazen's work on the road. They believed Hazen had hired natives along the frontier to participate in the work.[345]

While the war continued in other parts of the country, the northern frontier was relatively quiet for several months. The temperatures cooled. The leaves turned and fell. Going into November, the frontier was oddly quiet.

The British evaluated the work at Île aux Noix, and some men from the Twenty-Ninth Regiment were redeployed to St. Jean.[346] A substantial part of the unit remained on the isolated island and kept watchful eyes on Missisquoi Bay.

Later that month, the Americans sent John Brown as a scout to the Lamoille River. He departed from Jacob Bayley's settlement along the Connecticut River. Brown was gone nine days and traveled about sixty-six miles.[347]

The British launched a limited operation in November. Pittsford, Brandon and the surrounding towns suffered through yet another attack.[348] It started on November 20 and lasted for a few days. Homes were burned, colonial families were displaced and prisoners were taken. Approximately four hundred colonial militiamen were mustered as the enemy departed.

The war dragged on, and yet another winter approached.

Chapter 11

"HESSIANS, TORIES AND BRITS..."

1780

As January's cold weather gripped the region, companies of the Twenty-Ninth Regiment of Foot were still stationed at St. Jean. Some of the unit was still on the Vermont border, at Île aux Noix.[349] The lake and rivers were frozen over. Deep snows covered the ground. For some, it seemed as though the war had exited the region.

However, General Schuyler floated another Quebec invasion through the Champlain Valley in a letter to George Washington on January 16. He believed that the peninsulas to the west of Missisquoi Bay, the present-day town of Alburgh and the western edges of Swanton, would provide a secluded staging area. He explained that the isolated waters of Missisquoi would mask an invasion. The army could strike at Île aux Noix and St. Jean before the British organized a defense.[350] Washington considered the idea, but no action was taken.

On March 12, the little Vermont Republic needed funds. Land was available for settlement in the northern tier of the state. The towns of Westford, Jay, Richford, Montgomery, Berkshire and Enosburgh were organized, chartered and open for settlement. Some of the new Vermont towns were named after men who had served with Benedict Arnold, who was no longer in the Champlain Valley. He now commanded West Point and was about to be wooed over to the Crown by English lieutenant John André. Arnold's traitorous activities were not exposed for months, and even though he spent much of his career in the Champlain Valley, bled and nearly died here, no one suggested his name be given to any of the new towns. Enosburgh was granted in the name of Major General Roger Enos.[351] He had turned his back on Arnold in the deep woods of Maine during the cold weather of 1775. The town of Montgomery was named after General Richard Montgomery. The official charters were adopted about two months later.

With the war still raging elsewhere in the colonies, the rebels strengthened their position in the central part of the state. In March and April, the Board of War authorized the construction of yet another fort in Pittsford. It was meant to augment the existing three, Fort Mott, Fort Ranger and Fort Warren. It had a six-foot-deep trench that surrounded an eighteen-foot-high picketed wall.[352] When one of the soldiers assigned there was found shot and scalped, Ebenezer Allen dubbed the location Fort Vengeance.

The worries of central Vermont were justified, but locations to the north were targeted more frequently. The British sailed on the lake with their large ships, supporting gunboats and countless bateaux. This time, their sights were set on the western shores of Lake Champlain, where they sent raiding parties into the Mohawk Valley of New York. Alarms spread through the Green Mountains on May 30, and the Vermont Militia mustered near Fort Ticonderoga to help intercept returning British forces. By June 6, the British raid was over.[353]

General Bayley, still in Newbury, understood that raids were a constant danger and agreed to defensively upgrade a specific property in Peacham. Captain Aldrich oversaw the building of a ditch and the establishment of a blockhouse-like structure on property owned by Bayley.[354]

The late spring and early summer activity gave British agents cover to lay the seeds of dissent. Ethan Allen, who had returned from his captivity, was secretly approached with a proposal meant to draw Vermont away from the colonies. For three years now, Congress had not known how to treat the Vermont situation. It had more important problems to solve than intervening in land disputes between New York, New Hampshire and local settlers. The letter that Allen received while walking on the streets of Arlington was as serious as Benedict Arnold's communications with John André. If New Hampshire, New York or the other squabbling colonies would not recognize Vermont, the king of England would. Vermont must remain under the governance of the Crown but would be relieved of other colonies' land claims. The proposal was considered, but there were questions about territorial boundaries, especially lands in Upstate New York, east of the Hudson River.[355] This included Fort Ticonderoga, Crown Point and the land that led to the original conflict between New York and New Hampshire.

Another of Vermont's "Founding Fathers," Thomas Chittenden, sent out a boat under a flag of truce to the British fleet. He agreed, in principle, with the idea of an armistice.[356] Nothing substantial was immediately agreed to. The negotiations would unfold in the coming months.

North of the Green Mountains, the British were concerned about French Canadians with colonial sympathies. They suspected that some of them had sent information to American agents. During the final days of June, two Canadians were observed moving along the Quebec line. One was Anthony Gerard, the man Arnold used as a scout prior to the Battle of Valcour Island. The same man had been employed by Simon Metcalf. Scout teams aggressively scoured Missisquoi Bay and the Lake Champlain islands, looking for the men.[357]

In July 1780, the Americans actively scouted northward, near the Lamoille River. They sent John Martin, who had reconned the region the previous fall, along the winding waterway to a Mr. Brown's house.[358] His mission lasted nine days and was under the command of Colonel Whitcomb. A few days later, a Sergeant Bliss was killed along the same patrol route, and Martin was ordered back to the Lamoille. For another five days, he searched for the presence of the enemy. The American probing was likely connected to the work on the Hazen-Bayley Road. Meanwhile, on July 19, a native scout reported to the British that hundreds of Americans were working in the woods, closing in on the eastern portions of the Missisquoi River.[359]

That same month, the large British ships once again flexed their muscles on the lake. They escorted bateaux and canoes full of native and Tory raiders into the Champlain Valley. Once ashore near the town of Pittsford, they took local resident Isaac Matson captive and imprisoned him in Canada.[360] The warships remained on the lake, and the attacks continued. The old nemesis Roger Stevens returned, ambushing settlers and taking captives. The militia and garrisons were mustered, but there were no major confrontations.[361]

By September, the secret negotiations between the Vermont Republic and the English dragged on. The proposals would become known as the Haldimand Negotiations. Ideas were pitched to Vermont's leaders to peel the territory away from the rest of the colonies. One idea was to pay the salaries of some Vermont soldiers who had not received their Continental salaries for some time.[362]

The Crown decided that the people living in the Green Mountains needed a reminder that the war was still being waged. A large force of eight hundred men was assembled and brought to the Richelieu River. In the final days of the month, they sailed to Île aux Noix. Once again, the outpost at arm's reach from Missisquoi Bay was a staging area for a major military operation.[363]

The targets were Crown Point, Fort Ticonderoga and the blockhouses and garrisons of central Vermont and Lake George. This was a bold incursion, and a lot of men and resources were needed. The bulk of the force came from the Twenty-Ninth, Thirty-Fourth, Fifty-Third and Eighty-Fourth Regiments. Four hundred more came from other units. Various bands of natives, Loyalists and Quebec militia joined the soldiers at Île aux Noix.[364] An advanced group was sent over Lake Champlain, through the Green Mountains, as the rest of the force came together. This band of St. Regis Mohawks stalked settlers all the way to the town of Bethel, where Fort Fortitude was under construction. The natives struck and killed two locals, David Stone and Silas Cleaveland.[365] The British knew the colonials had a meager presence in the region. When they moved south, there was no organized resistance. On the night of September 29, they camped on Isle La Motte. The larger vessels were tucked close to shore, and the soldiers camped on the island.[366] Christopher Carleton led the attack.

When the British once again asserted control over Lake Champlain in 1780, they sailed by the southern tip of Isle La Motte. *Photo by Armand Messier and Northern Vermont Aerial Photography.*

The flotilla, led by the *Maria*, returned to the hotly contested forts, already the heart of so many operations during the war. On October 6, the British occupied Crown Point, but it was no longer much of a strategic location. It had been abandoned by the Americans and used only as a temporary base. The next day, the British occupied Ticonderoga once again.[367]

The show of force coincided with the resumption of the Haldimand Negotiations. The Allens represented Vermont, while Justus Sherwood forwarded the king's positions. Officially, the meetings were about an exchange of prisoners. Few people knew about them. Proposals were exchanged. From the Allens' perspective, Ethan Allen would command the forces in the region, and Vermont would have a separate government from the Crown.[368] Haldimand, through his associates, demanded that the government be appointed by the king. The British wanted to occupy Bennington and, with the support of the Allens, march with the Green Mountain Boys to Albany. Ultimately, the Allens continued to explore the potential reunion with the mother country as a negotiation tactic against the other colonies.

On the west side of the lake, the British forces continued to operate near old Fort St. Ann, Fort Edward and Lake George. They burned the homes of suspected rebels. Various skirmishes, scouting missions and pursuits persisted until the British force returned to Fort Ticonderoga on October 15.[369]

Part of the fleet sailed north to the mouth of the Onion River. Richard Houghton of the Fifty-Third Regiment of Foot led about 250 Kahnawake Mohawk and Abenaki warriors into the Green Mountains.[370] They followed the path of the Onion River inland and went all the way to Royalton, along the eastern edge of the state. On October 16, they attacked and took twenty-seven prisoners. They passed through present-day Randolph and captured Zadock Steele the next day. That night, Vermont militia caught up with the natives, and a firefight erupted in the darkness. The natives took the prisoners and vanished. For the next three days, the war party followed the Onion River and returned westward. On October 20, they reached the mouth of the river, where they hid their birch-bark canoes and batteaux. The prisoners were brought onto the *Carleton*.[371] The British passed the southern tip of Grand Isle and moved to rejoin Carleton's fleet on their return journey.[372]

As late as October 25, the *Maria* still operated around Crown Point, collecting Loyalist refugees who sought the safety of Quebec.[373] Meanwhile, the Vermont government inked the charters for Grand Isle, North Hero and South Hero; the land was a reward for men who fought for the colonial cause.

The British were prepared to return to Quebec but received orders to remain on the lake. They were not happy with the Allens' negotiations, and warships visibly controlling the lake was a blunt reminder that the war was still on.

On October 26, the flotilla neared Ticonderoga; a few days later, British soldiers reoccupied Vermont soil. The agents of the Crown showed their flag at Mount Independence.[374] No major engagements took place, but their mere presence sent a message.

They remained in the southern regions of the lake well into November. On the eleventh, several British ships took on Loyalists at Skenesborough. The refugees had seen the writing on the wall. England had stopped putting resources into defeating the rebels in the northern colonies. However, these residents remained loyal and left their lands in Upstate New York behind. The next day, the fleet was heading north. American intelligence was aware that large numbers of enemy soldiers were at the mouth of the Onion River around this time.[375]

They sailed by Grand Isle, North Hero, Isle La Motte and Alburgh. They encountered ice in some of the shallow bays on the west side of the lake. That night, they spent the evening just over the border, on Ash Island, within the confined waters of the Richelieu River. Not quite home, they returned to Île aux Noix and St. Jean the next day.[376]

On November 12, Simon Metcalf, presumably back on his Missisquoi property, petitioned Quebec authorities to cut firewood. Metcalf didn't think he was asking for anything new; he just wanted to continue an agreement he'd once had with Guy Carleton.[377]

As the British finished flexing their muscles on the lake, they increased their forces occupying Point au Fer. Roger Stevens and several recruits were sent to monitor anything moving on the water and observe the Lake Champlain islands.[378]

By November, George Washington had been made aware of the secret negotiations between Vermont and the British in Quebec.[379] Locally, Governor Chittenden hoped the continued talks might be a way of securing the release of the recent Royalton Raid prisoners.[380]

The temporary truce went forward, at least within the Green Mountains. Vermont leaders agreed to it because they were concerned about colonial inability to protect the frontier.[381] The potential for prisoner exchanges continued to be the public reason for the meetings. Ira Allen and Joseph Fay represented Vermont. They traveled north to meet with Justus Sherwood. The discussions were to be held in Quebec, but when they reached the area of

Ira Allen participated in the secret Haldimand Negotiations. *Courtesy of the Vermont Historical Society.*

Maquam Bay and East Bay, they found the ice already forming, obstructing their boat journey.[382] They reached the area west of present-day Swanton and St. Albans before returning home.

By December 17, Metcalf had settled back on his Missisquoi property, cutting enough wood to keep his family warm, and he planned on renewing his economic activities. To Metcalf's surprise, the provincial government suddenly seemed open to hearing his concerns about events during the war. He had just lived through half a decade of raids, scouts, theft and imprisonment. A British official, a Mr. Mathews, wanted to know more about individuals who took advantage of Metcalf and those who had stolen from his property.[383]

On Christmas, Metcalf thanked the man. He took full advantage of the avenue of communication and gave Mathews all the information he had. Metcalf complained that people with access to Haldimand and the Quebec government were responsible, and he had not been given a chance to rebut any charges. A personal interview had been requested but was never granted. Metcalf noted that the charges against him had never been brought by the military. Stepping lightly but being honest, Metcalf asked if he could restart his sawmill. To his dismay, another private interest had been given the authority to harvest wood in the area, with the permission of Colonel Barry St. Leger.[384]

Metcalf wanted things to go back to the way they had been before the war.

Britain's overall war effort continued to shift away from the northern colonies. It gave much attention to the southern colonies but left enough forces in Quebec to maintain a firm military presence.

Chapter 12

"AFTER SIX YEARS OF WAR"

1781

As winter began, Simon Metcalf wrote in a small bound journal from what was left of his settlement in Prattsburgh. He observed the increased economic activity of the British presence near Missisquoi Bay. He understood the potential of Lake Champlain and the surrounding forests. In the final days of December, he observed nearly three hundred axmen in the employ of the British, felling large oaks and other trees. Most of the timber was never used in North America. It was processed by British military and sent to economic interests in England.[385] The lumber was dragged over the ice by teams of horses and oxen or put aside until spring, when boats could retrieve it.

His communications with authorities in Quebec showed someone barely containing simmering frustrations. On January 25, he again wrote Mathews. Cutting wood for his own stove was fine, but Quebec did not want him restarting his sawmill. At the same time, he noted that there were two separate entities cutting timber on his land. One group was the English government. The other was aligned with what Metcalf thought were "persons of the worst description." He had asked a lawyer to initiate a formal complaint; Metcalf wanted nearly five hundred recently cut white oak trees seized and turned over to him. He again asked the authorities if he could cut timber. He also requested to cut hay in the coming summer for what farm animals he had left. Boxed into a corner and hoping he had not pressed too strongly, he specifically mentioned that Barry St. Leger and Alexander Fraser, two British officers deployed around St. Jean and Île aux Noix, were taking wood from his land.

As an indication that many considered Quebec a safe haven, more Tories entered the region. This time it wasn't to join the military but to settle down. In February, northern Alburgh, right along the forty-fifth parallel, was settled by Tory refugees.[386]

At the same time, British leadership sent Ethan Allen and the Vermont leadership another letter. This time, they agreed to nearly all of the stipulations the Vermonters had raised over the previous several months.[387] Thomas Chittenden and the Allens still refused to agree to anything, except to meet again.

The war and the scouting missions continued.

In February, the colonials dispatched Solomon Cushman, Elias Stephens and Joshua Spers on a seven-day mission from Norwich, all the way up to the Onion River.[388] These men operated just opposite of Roger Stevens and his Loyalists, who were on guard at Point au Fer. They had spent the last four months manning, patrolling and spying on the region from the White House.[389]

As spring warmth got closer, the British started the initial construction of a blockhouse in North Hero.[390] This was a blatant show of strength and a total disregard for Vermont territory.

On the eastern side of the Green Mountains, British forces led by Tory Azariah Pritchard scouted near the town of Peacham on March 8. They encountered Colonel Thomas Johnson, Jonathan Elkins and Jacob Page, whom they took prisoner and brought back to Quebec.[391]

As winter finally loosened its grip, Quebec woodsmen continued to descend into the Champlain Valley. The three hundred axmen Metcalf had observed were still hard at work, dropping valuable oak for the mother country's economy. The ice thawed, and significant numbers of British craft were all over the lake, ferrying logs to Quebec ports, and then on to Europe.[392]

On May 1, Ethan Allen's birthday, a party of about twenty Vermonters sailed north toward the forty-fifth parallel. Ira Allen was the leader of the group. The secret aspects of the Haldimand Negotiations continued, this time in Quebec. Allen's party moved along the Lake Champlain islands and covered the very same ground colonial soldiers had traversed six years earlier. They arrived at Île aux Noix and stayed for several days. The easiest item to discuss, that which was public, was the transfer of prisoners. They also covered the continuation of the truce. The British still wanted the Green Mountains to return to the jurisdiction of the king, and after seventeen days of proposals, they were informed that the Vermont legislature would convene in May.[393] During the talks, Ira Allen took in just how close they were to the Vermont frontier. He looked southeast, toward home, and knew that the waters of Missisquoi Bay were just a few miles distant. Ira's interest in the northwest corner of Vermont would play out in the coming years, and it was not entirely selfless.

On May 14, Jacob Bayley made overtures to the St. Francis tribe to the north. A number of tribesmen had already come over to the colonial cause and were employed by the American army. Bayley made offerings of clothing. He wanted to lure the natives as scouts. Just days earlier, his men had found three enemy deserters following the Missisquoi River eastward, away from the British-controlled areas of Lake Champlain. The men informed Bayley of the British blockhouse under construction on North Hero.[394]

The Loyalists operating at Point au Fer were ordered to conduct more harassment operations in May. Native warriors and their Tory allies snuck down to Fort Vengeance and launched a quick attack. With the fort secure, the colonial commander received a request for a brief meeting. Captain Benjamin Cooley met with the Tory, Roger Stevens. Stevens claimed he was doing what he could to protect the residents of Otter Creek, understanding how much of a toll the attacks had on his former friends and neighbors. He claimed that he was making sure prisoners were being handled with care and respect.[395]

On June 3, British eyes on the lake were alerted to an American scouting mission in Missisquoi Bay. Approximately two dozen colonials were there, led by two natives. There was no engagement, but the rebels got close enough to St. Jean to raise concern. At the same time, Benjamin Whitcomb was coordinating with Bayley, who was gathering more information from sources at the village of St. Francis.[396]

Meanwhile, the British continued their small raids. Their native allies descended upon Fort Vengeance again, this time led by Chief Tomo of the Caughnawagas. Gunfire was exchanged, the attack was repulsed and the chief was wounded in the right leg.[397] At the end of June, British agents were all over Missisquoi Bay, scouring the woods for two more deserters. A Mr. Rose and Jessie Brown tried to move across the forty-fifth parallel undetected. Eventually, they were found and brought back to Quebec.[398]

Quebec officials finally responded to Metcalf's plea to cut hay. After months of delay, Mathews finally gave Metcalf permission to cut hay in Prattsburgh. Unfortunately, the information came on July 2, already well into the growing season. Mathews also informed him that his complaints about St. Leger—and now Twiss, the leading engineer working on upgrades at Île aux Noix—needed to be handled by the courts.[399] Metcalf responded immediately. He complained about the establishment of a sawmill at Lacolle Mills, on the western side of the Richelieu in Quebec. Even if he could process lumber, the new mill would undercut any production managed in Missisquoi Bay.

In July, the British work continued on the North Hero blockhouse. Justus Sherwood and a group of loyalists oversaw the building of the fortification.[400] While shovels moved dirt and logs were laid, the Haldimand Negotiations continued. The British vessel *Royal George* was the transport ship for prisoner exchanges. It passed Alburgh's Windmill point to collect prisoners of war. It returned the length of the lake and, at the height of summer, returned the locals to Vermont.[401] Vermont released some of its British prisoners.

In Missisquoi Bay, Metcalf pleaded for his livelihood. He inquired if he could rebuild his small mill and deliver lumber at prices that would keep him working but would not provide a profit. He tried to grow enough hay for four workhorses. Metcalf provided a property map of the boundaries of Prattsburgh to Twiss, but the engineer did not care. Metcalf's pleas were ignored.

As peak summer arrived, British commanders worried about any American movement through Missisquoi Bay and the Missisquoi River.[402] They ordered constant scouting. Those soldiers were witness to the growing problems Metcalf had to deal with. In early August, hordes of insects ravaged his hay crop. He still wanted to cut small amounts of wood and begged British authorities to call off the teams of engineers cutting timber for the Île aux Noix fortifications. They were still cutting trees on his land. Mathews, his contact in Quebec, informed Metcalf that the government would purchase all of the wood that he could provide, but that the Missisquoi sawmill would not be restarted. The news prompted Metcalf to travel to Quebec to make his case in front of the authorities. He visited at the wrong time, as the British were preparing more incursions on Lake Champlain. Frustrated, Metcalf asked for a bateau on August 18 to return to Prattsburgh, but he was not allowed to leave.[403] In a bitter twist that brought Metcalf no reprieve, engineer Twiss filed paperwork addressing one of Metcalf's grievances. Iron ore had indeed been harvested without compensation for Metcalf. However, Twiss pointed out that it happened prior to his coming on as the head engineer, and nothing could be done about it.[404]

The organizational activity Metcalf witnessed in Quebec, what he saw that led to his detainment, unfolded shortly afterward. The British returned to the lake and once again wanted to occupy Fort Ticonderoga.

To maintain control of northern Lake Champlain, the British constructed a blockhouse on North Hero. *Artwork by Josh Sinz.*

Colonel Barry St. Leger commanded the cobbled-together companies from the reorganized Twenty-Ninth, Thirty-First and Forty-Fourth Light Infantry companies. A larger contingent of the Thirty-Fourth Battalion participated in the venture. A few Loyalist units gladly went along for the ride. The task force stopped off at Point au Fer to reinforce that garrison. Nearly seventy bateaux were involved with the mission. They all sailed directly past Alburgh, Isle La Motte and the islands.[405] While the British occupied Lake Champlain, the Haldimand Negotiations continued.

Simon Metcalf was released shortly afterward. His return to Missisquoi was an opportunity for the British. They likely fed him incorrect military information regarding troop movements, commanding officers and ship strength, knowing he might relay it to colonials prowling the frontier. Finally, during the dog days of August, Metcalf started cutting wood.[406]

The Americans sent scouts John Martin and Lieutenant Henry Lovel through the Green Mountains to Metcalf's settlement during the British occupation of the lake. In an example of the circumstances of someone's life only getting worse, the colonials demanded Metcalf accompany them to investigate enemy activity.[407] Metcalf's son and three French Canadian workers were also seized but released on September 1. They traveled for points farther south. During his forced service, Metcalf was allowed to write a letter to his wife. It was handed to her by the three Frenchmen who had been released earlier.[408]

To make matters worse for the Metcalfs, British operatives were hiding in the woods. They were immediately aware of Metcalf's absence and sent men to the Missisquoi River to assess the situation. They took his Canadian workers back to their guard houses and imprisoned them in Quebec. Loyalist Azeriah Pritchard was sent into the bay to keep tabs on American activity and await the possible return of Metcalf.[409] After a few days, Metcalf and his son were released by the colonials and returned home.

While Metcalf's misfortune along the Missisquoi continued, the Allens were still dragging the Haldimand Negotiations along. Perhaps gauging just how much support the British might put into the talks, Ira Allen floated a plan for "Greater Vermont." The Allens thought they might be able to stack the Vermont Assembly with representatives favorable to annexing disputed parts of New Hampshire and New York.[410] St. Leger returned to Quebec with the proposal in hand. However, events in Virginia, with the possible defeat of the British at Yorktown, prompted Ira Allen to delay any outcome of the talks.

Catherine Metcalf, alone in Missisquoi Bay due to both warring sides seizing her husband in a matter of weeks, was desperate. She wrote to Mathews, her husband's contact in Quebec, and asked him to pay on an account that had been previously established.[411]

When her husband returned to Missisquoi, it wasn't for long. On September 17, the British descended on his property and arrested him again. They had never been interested in his freedom, property rights or economic activity. Even Mathews, the court contact, was unforgiving. On September 20, Mathews bluntly responded to Mrs. Metcalf and declared that her husband had aided the enemy. By late September, British intelligence agents were congratulating each other, as Metcalf's August release had indeed been a ruse to feed disinformation to the Americans.[412] The family's permission to cut wood was revoked. At the end of September, Metcalf once again pleaded with British authorities and tried to explain the circumstances that just kept getting worse.[413]

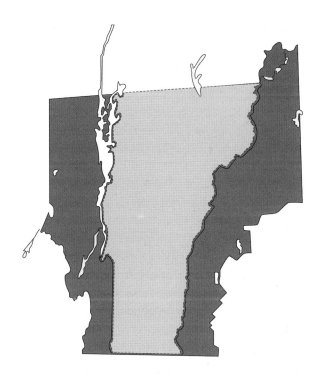

As part of the secret Haldimand Negotiations, the idea of "Greater Vermont" was briefly floated. *Artwork by Lindsay DiDio.*

While the Haldimand talks lingered on, the prisoner exchanges continued. One was orchestrated at Skenesborough at the end of September.[414] Another happened a week later. On October 5, Colonel Thomas Johnson, who had been held prisoner at St. Jean, was paroled, released and allowed to return home.[415]

The British occupation of Fort Ticonderoga and southern Lake Champlain lasted until November, when, to their surprise, word arrived of Lord Cornwallis's defeat at Yorktown. The men and boats returned to Quebec on November 15. They brought the news of the defeat with them.[416]

Chapter 13

"FROM THE FRONTIER TO STATEHOOD"

1782 and Beyond

In the first weeks of February 1782, the British took advantage of snow cover and kept track of American activity. Two scouting missions departed Quebec to check on the Bayley-Hazen military road. One moved across the forty-fifth parallel, got to the Missisquoi River and then traveled to the Loyalist blockhouse at North Hero. The other went farther inland and detected no activity where the Americans had ceased construction on the road.[417] Justus Sherwood, who was stationed at the blockhouse, reported that the lake was completely frozen over, all the way to Crown Point.

Hostilities had been paused for a few months, but locals and military men were not sure if they were enemies. In February, General Friedrich Riedesel, now in command of the British and Hessian soldiers in the area, toured British-occupied lands in New York and Vermont. He spent February 26 at Point au Fer. That night, a fire in a woodstove spread and damaged one of the blockhouses. The flames spread to the main building, which was also damaged. The next morning, against the extreme cold of winter, the men set about making repairs. Riedesel had military matters on his agenda and ordered that if the North Hero blockhouse were ever attacked, the men should retreat to Point au Fer.[418]

Simon Metcalf, traveling between Quebec and his property in Missisquoi Bay, wrote to American authorities that the land north of the forty-fifth parallel was ripe for the taking. His allegiances had been put to rest by his recent treatment in Quebec. Metcalf suggested that a winter campaign might put the British at a significant disadvantage.[419] He speculated about

General Riedesel became the commander of the British, Loyalist and Hessian forces stationed at Île aux Noix. *Courtesy of the Library of Congress.*

British troop movements during a future American invasion, and he provided details about the number of ships operating on the lake.

Vermont was still involved in the Haldimand Negotiations but had little reason to embrace them.[420] On February 28, written communications passed between the two governments.[421] With the defeat of General Cornwallis during the fall, the British still wanted to pluck Vermont away from the colonies. Vermonters were trying to quash land claims of New York and New Hampshire, and the British desired to keep the negotiations alive. More overtures were penned in March and April.

Meanwhile, the northern frontier was far from quiet. The British sent out scouts to monitor activity along the dormant Bayley-Hazen military road. At the same time, tensions mounted in Missisquoi Bay, and twelve British soldiers were sent to protect the woodcutters.[422]

In the spring of 1782, with the overall negotiations stalled, the British used strong-arm tactics to make Champlain Valley leaders understand military reality. Large numbers of soldiers were deployed to Île aux Noix.[423] Their presence was rationalized by stating that they feared American military aggression might come through the Champlain Valley. And if New York authorities decided to pursue their land claims in the Green Mountains, the English hoped Vermonters would see the troops as warding off New York aggression.

As the weather warmed and the fighting was left behind, Jacob Bayley noted that settlers were moving into the area of the Lamoille and Onion Rivers.[424] On May 31, the British government authorized further timber cutting in Missisquoi Bay.[425] It wasn't Simon Metcalf doing the cutting.

An uneasy peace, of sorts, settled on the Champlain Valley, but the plots and schemes of war were still in play. In early June, a group of Tories set out for Newbury with the intention of capturing Jacob Bayley and bringing him back to Quebec. The scheme was hatched by Azariah Pritchard and a Captain Breckenridge, Loyalists who had left New England for Quebec during the war. Pritchard first contacted Thomas Johnson, who had recently been a prisoner. His contact with Johnson was rooted in deceit. Acting on orders from Haldimand and the British army, he communicated that the king had called off native attacks as a gesture to get Vermont to consider rejoining the empire. Pritchard wanted to plant seeds of doubt between Jacob Bayley and Thomas Chittenden, who had political differences. The Tory mentioned the plot to kidnap Bayley, thinking Johnson's time in prison had corrupted his loyalties. The attempt unfolded on June 15 but was not successful. Knowing the War for Independence was close to over, Bayley may have let the assailants escape.[426] That month, British warships were on the lake again, traveling as far south as Skenesborough, involved in yet another prisoner transfer. George Avery, taken prisoner during the Royalton Raid in October 1781, was finally released.[427]

Simon Metcalf was back in Swanton and, with the fighting over, tried to support his family. He wrote to the Continental Congress and hoped the final peace treaty would include a provision that Americans would get access to roads and waterways on the Quebec border.[428] Metcalf also observed that there was just a small detachment stationed at Île aux Noix, no longer a full regiment.[429]

With the war officially over, for the first time in three years no ship sailed Lake Champlain with the intent of raiding north or south. No soldier loaded his musket expecting to point it at an emerging enemy. One report filed by men still stationed at Point au Fer noted that parts of the stone house were falling into disrepair.[430]

The tense peace featured defensive work by the British. Engineers developed further plans to expand the emplacements on Île au Noix.[431] The work on the structures and redoubts began during the warm weather of 1782. German General Riedesel, whose troops were still stationed in Quebec, received a long-term reassignment to the outpost.[432]

At one point in late August, Haldimand considered sending Hessian soldiers down the Alburgh peninsula, straight onto Isle La Motte. Île aux Noix was to have been the launching point for the operation, but he never followed through with the orders.[433]

As fall descended on the Champlain Valley, the air became more crisp. The first leaves turned. Riedesel, well aware that his forces still occupied land that clearly belonged to the former thirteen colonies, recommended a substantial resupply of Point au Fer and the North Hero blockhouse. He requested supplies for one hundred soldiers be sent to the White House and that food for sixty soldiers be sent to North Hero.[434] While passing away the time at Île aux Noix, Riedesel wrote many letters to his wife, who was living along the St. Lawrence.[435] As he put pen to paper, his soldiers kept a watchful eye on Missisquoi Bay and Windmill Point.

Riedesel had to deal with a missing scout in December. No one was sure if the man had defected, so they sent out squads to assess the situation. During the last week of December, as temperatures plunged, the concerned soldiers questioned the woodcutters felling trees along Missisquoi Bay. According to them, the scout had proceeded farther south.[436]

In March 1783, Ebenezer Allen and other veterans awarded lands in the Lake Champlain islands visited to look at their property.[437] Ira Allen and his associates settled down in the town of Colchester.[438] At the same time, British soldiers and Loyalists had trouble controlling the settlement of the population that had fled to Quebec. Many of them believed the northern Champlain Valley would be a nice place to settle. Around March 7, three Loyalists were seized around the Onion River, men who thought that land was available for agents of the Crown.[439] In the spring, the British still worked to upgrade Île au Noix.[440]

Peacetime life started to expand. Ebenezer Allen operated a ferry between the Lake Champlain islands and the edge of Colchester Point.[441]

Not surprisingly, the Haldimand Negotiations broke down. Haldimand wanted more negotiations, but the Allens refused to respond.

As the snows melted, green returned to the land, and the British occupation of parts of the Champlain Valley remained a sticking point for Vermont and New York. The fighting in the region had stopped almost a year and a half earlier.

The British maintained their forts at Point au Fer and Dutchman's Point on North Hero. The White House was commanded by Captain de Rochambeau. Even though the peace treaty was signed in 1783, Britain was not going to allow Quebec to be threatened.[442] Whoever controlled the lake controlled the fortifications, and the British taunted American shipping with the presence of the schooner *Maria*. It maintained a position in and around Grand Isle county and often bullied legitimate commercial ventures.

As the British relied on Île aux Noix, they continued to make upgrades to the island. Engineers planned on the construction of five redoubts, small structures meant to provide protection in the event of an assault. These would complement and augment the existing fort. Three had been completed by the end of the summer.[443] They were connected by a trench that emerged from the fort.[444] The wood for these projects came from the area of Missisquoi Bay.

With the Revolution in the rearview mirror, George Washington visited Fort Ticonderoga.[445] As the former commanding general enjoyed his victory lap, Loyalists tried to figure out where and how they were going to live. Quebec wanted to usher many Loyalists north to a region on the St. Lawrence River, but a small group came to see Missisquoi Bay as a desirable place to settle. Haldimand and others had no desire to see this happen. Natives still inhabited the territory, and the land around Missisquoi Bay literally was the physical border with the former colonies. As 1783 ended and 1784 began, a defiant group claimed it had purchased the old Indian title. By March, it had moved into the area at the northern edges of Swanton, Highgate and present-day Franklin.[446]

William Gilliland, who had been the New York landowner north of Ticonderoga prior to the Revolution and lost much of his land because of the war, petitioned to get the British to abandon Point au Fer. English soldiers still occupied the point across from Alburgh, and the request went nowhere. On April 15, Vermont put in a similar inquiry. Thomas Chittenden wrote to the Quebec government that, with peace achieved, the abandonment of the British blockhouse in North Hero was appropriate.[447]

In an ironic twist, Levi Allen, one of the lesser-known members of the family, lost his claim of the town of Swanton in a tax sale. The person who took advantage of his misfortune was his brother Ira. With the transaction, Ira Allen owned most of the land around the Missisquoi Bay.[448] In early May, another tense moment unfolded when groups of Loyalists defied the Quebec government and finalized their plans to move east of Missisquoi Bay, literally on the colonial border.[449]

On July 5, Ebenezer Allen, representing the state of Vermont, wrote to Simon Metcalf in Swanton. Allen's cousins were not happy that Metcalf had returned to try to work his former land. The Allens considered the original New York land claims obsolete. Ebenezer let Metcalf know he was planning a visit to execute the laws of the young Republic of Vermont.[450] Metcalf's misfortune continued. The tension around who owned the land in Swanton increased exponentially in September. Small bands of Abenaki, who had moved their families away to avoid the fighting, returned to the region between Missisquoi and Rock Rivers.[451]

By 1785, without a war going on, the British garrison at St. Jean was in disrepair. The soldiers on guard duty needed activity to pass the downtime. At the end of April, the ice was melted. In early May, some of the troops from St. Jean and Île aux Noix decided to go fishing on Lake Champlain. They had fought for the territory less than a decade before. John Enys and

The Missisquoi River near where it empties into Missisquoi Bay. After everything Simon Metcalf had been through, Ira Allen took his land after the American Revolution. *Photograph by the author.*

his associates caught fish off Isle La Motte on May 13. The next day, they headed south and west toward the Saranac River. They encountered the American settlement there. They caught many perch and shared their catch with their Yankee neighbors.[452] The visitors fished Cumberland Bay and then the coast of Grand Isle until May 17. A messenger from Quebec approached; the group was being redeployed and needed to return to base. They remained one more night.[453]

Life was returning to normal. A small ferry was established between North Hero and Grand Isle. Near the border, Americans and occupying Brits and Loyalists now lived close to one another.[454]

By the mid-1780s, Quebec's English government acknowledged it had a problem with the Loyalists, many settling too close to the former colonies. One group settled along the Chazy River in Upstate New York. The eastern shores of Missisquoi Bay, within the present-day Vermont towns of Swanton, Highgate and Franklin, developed a significant Loyalist population.[455] The settlement issues were terribly complicated near the Missisquoi River. Another group of Frenchmen and Abenaki returned in 1786. Tensions flared. Settlers' homes were threatened. Colonel Ebenezer Allen was sent to Swanton with a small detachment of soldiers and patrolled the Missisquoi River to make sure things did not get out of hand.[456] Ira Allen was set to benefit mightily if events quieted down, and he didn't want Natives scaring away potential settlers. In court, he claimed the Natives were not from the area, that they were from the Quebec village of St. Francis. Allen took advantage of their lack of legal status, and since he was of the Allen clan, he didn't have to worry whether the courts would side against him.[457]

Later, in 1787, British soldiers were still stationed at the Richelieu forts. The trading vessels moving over Lake Champlain encountered them as they moved beyond the border towns into Quebec. In October and November, English soldier John Enys was stationed at the forts once again. Almost a decade had unfolded since his first deployment in the area. Captain Stephen Pearl owned a schooner that docked at St. Jean. He ferried well-to-do travelers onto the lake. On one trip, snow and wind held the party up, and they were forced to put ashore about two hundred yards north of the border, very near the forty-fifth parallel. Old paths to Missisquoi Bay were observed by the travelers. They got underway again, and as they ventured south, they saw the British outpost on Point au Fer.[458] On November 5, they saw Point au Roche, on the New York side, and found that Moses Hazen had settled there. They noted that Hazen had not aged well and seemed to be living in rather rough conditions. That night, they crossed the lake and stayed at the home of Jedediah Hyde, where they were treated well and given pumpkin beer.[459]

As the years passed, Vermont's frontier wilderness attracted settlers and investors, especially along the northern tier of the state. Landowners and surveyors evaluated the border markers established prior to the Revolution. Errors were discovered that altered the boundaries of the state. Collins and Valentine, cutting through miles of wilderness in the early 1770s, had been inaccurate in their measurements. Along the eastern boundary of the Green Mountains, where Vermont stretches to the Connecticut River, the Canadian border line was twelve miles too far south.[460] The error was minor on Vermont's Lake Champlain shores, but the measurement mistakes contributed to land issues that involved the Missisquoi Loyalists. They had used the forty-fifth parallel boundary when they settled in the Rock River area of Highgate.

In 1788, Colonel Ebenezer Allen returned to the banks of the Missisquoi River with a small detachment of soldiers to make sure tensions between returning Abenaki, long-displaced French setters and locals did not boil over.[461]

The next year, those tensions were on the decline and Ethan Allen died unceremoniously. If the leaders of states and countries were still cold with the ongoing border disputes, the attitude of the locals had started to melt. British officers on the *Maria*, which still sailed back and forth between North Hero and Point au Fer, developed friendly relations with many locals. In one instance, they sent an early settler of Champlain, New York, a bag of apples. As relationships developed, British officers sailed a smaller boat up the Chazy River and were social with residents. More visits happened, and the tensions waned.[462]

Vermont was admitted into the United States in 1791. Circumstances remained unsettled as the British military maintained garrisons at the White House on Point au Fer and the blockhouse on North Hero. Even at this late date, British planners still considered erecting an artillery battery to strengthen their hold on the Point au Fer peninsula.[463] Vermont's admission into the United States did not impress the British, who meddled in the affairs of the town of Alburgh that year. Samuel Mott and Captain Marvin were elected justices of the peace. English troops were concerned that Vermont or U.S. law might be applied to their forces south of the forty-fifth parallel. They sent twelve soldiers into Alburgh and arrested Mott and Marvin. The two men were eventually released, but the message was clear. American or Vermont authority would not extend to British military personnel. Another point of frustration was the British presence at Windmill Point.[464]

The economy on the lake was dependent on sailing ships. Two commerce vessels were built at the docks in Burlington in the spring of 1794. They were the *Dolphin* and the *Burlington Packet*.[465]

While an uncomfortable calm settled over the Champlain Valley, the British still occupied slivers of American soil. On the lake, their armed vessels were an obstacle to American merchants wanting to transact business in Montreal, the largest, closest market. The *Maria*, even with the Revolution now a decade in the past, fired its guns on at least one trading vessel. Its last year of service was 1794, but the British did not abandon their naval presence on the lake. Another large vessel, the *Royal Edward*, which had sixteen cannons, was launched to show who still controlled the northern regions.[466] However, old enemies were stationed on the border, and they interacted and became cordial. One specific case involved Captain Steel of the *Royal Edward*. He was friendly with and then married Nancy Griggs of Alburgh, whose father had been a Tory and settled at Windmill Point after the Revolution. The ceremony was held at her parents' home.[467]

Jay's Treaty was signed and went into effect in 1796. At that point, the British relinquished control of Point au Fer in New York and the Dutchman's Point blockhouse in North Hero. Their final departure ended the post–Revolutionary War era in northern Vermont.

Postscript

LOOKING BACK

I t was a great honor to conduct research and write this book. Obviously, these pages are not meant to rehash extensive histories that have been written by other historians. The flavor of this book is entirely local, and where appropriate, I wove in references to the larger flow of the Revolutionary War.

The historic marker for the Bayley-Hazen blockhouse in Greensboro. *Photograph by the author.*

I expect Vermont will get a significant amount of attention as the 250th anniversary of the Revolution arrives in 2025. I cannot describe to you the enjoyment I feel in discovering that my home area was so intimately woven into such significant events.

Teaching and writing books at the same time is often difficult. I love my job as a high school history teacher. I can cover so much interesting and unique local history. It is a joy to share what I research with my students, as I feel they are receiving authentic information and can learn about their home areas. I don't expect my interest in Simon Metcalf's sawmill to compete with the latest TikTok video, but I try. I continue to build positive relationships with students and find the time to do worthy research.

Thank you for reading.

NOTES

Chapter 1

1. Allen, *History of the State of Vermont*, 23.
2. Shattuck, *Rebel and the Tory*.
3. Ibid.
4. Lampee, "Missisquoi Loyalists."
5. Randall, *Ethan Allen*.
6. Shattuck, *Rebel and the Tory*.
7. Perry, *History of the Town of Swanton*.
8. Lampee, "Missisquoi Loyalists."
9. Huden, *Indian Troubles in Early Vermont*.
10. Palmer, *History of Lake Champlain*.
11. Perry, *History of the Town of Swanton*.
12. Randall, *Ethan Allen*.
13. Myrick, *State Papers of Vermont*, 256.

Chapter 2

14. Nople, "Original Swanton Grant."
15. Myrick, *State Papers of Vermont*, 256.
16. Ibid., 272.
17. Perry, *History of the Town of Swanton*.

18. Enys, *American Journals of John Enys*, 326.

19. Myrick, *State Papers of Vermont*, 258.

20. Mayo, *Forty-Fifth Parallel*.

21. Freeman, *Documents of the Senate*, 19.

22. Mayo, *Forty-Fifth Parallel*, 261.

23. Freeman, *Documents of the Senate*, 20.

24. Fay, *Vermont's Ebenezer Allen*, 153.

25. Allen, *History of the State of Vermont*, 32, 33.

26. Fay, *Vermont's Ebenezer Allen*, 104.

27. Ibid., 129.

28. Bennet, *Few Lawless Vagabonds*, 43.

29. Hemenway, *Vermont Historical Gazeteer*, 290.

30. Everest, *Point Au Fer on Lake Champlain*, 13.

31. Cubbison, *American Northern Theater Army*.

32. Everst, *Point Au Fer on Lake Champlain*.

33. Ibid., 13, 14.

34. Hemenway, *Vermont Historical Gazeteer*, 701.

35. Randall, *Benedict Arnold*, 76.

36. Allen, *History of the State of Vermont*, 40.

37. Bellico, *Journeys in War and Peace*, 192.

38. Randall, *Benedict Arnold*, 109.

39. Nelson, *Benedict Arnold's Navy*, 18.

40. Underwood, "Indian and Tory Raids," 207.

Chapter 3

41. Fay, *Vermont's Ebenezer Allen*, 68.

42. Gauthier, *Siege of the Moses Pierson Blockhouse*.

43. Randall, *Benedict Arnold*, 83.

44. Ibid., 85.

45. Bellico, *Sales and Steam in the Mountains*.

46. Allen, *History of the State of Vermont*, 42.

47. Randall, *Benedict Arnold*, 101.

48. Everest, *Point Au Fer on Lake Champlain*, 16.

49. Nelson, *Benedict Arnold's Navy*, 43.

50. Randall, *Benedict Arnold*, 105.

51. Ibid., 108.

52. Everest, *Point Au Fer on Lake Champlain*, 15.

53. Charbonneau, *Fortifications of Île Aux Noix*, 68.

54. Randall, *Benedict Arnold*, 110.

55. Allen, *History of the State of Vermont*, 44.

56. Cubbison, *American Northern Theater Army*, 9.

57. Randall, *Benedict Arnold*, 147.

58. General Schuyler to the Continental Congress, July 27, 1775.

59. An Account of the Voyage of Captain Remember Baker, 1775.

60. Brymner, *Report on Canadian Archives*, 908.

61. Major John Brown to Governour Trumbull, August 14, 1775.

62. Wells, Journal of 1775, 232–48.

63. Report of Jas. Stewart, August 3, 1775.

64. Deposition of John Duguid, August 2, 1775.

65. Deposition of John Shatforth, August 2, 1775.

66. Paper delivered Major-General Schuyler by Captain Smith, August 2, 1775.

67. "Phillip Schuyler, Letter to George Washington," August 6, 1775.

68. Wells, Journal of 1775, 249.

69. American War for Indepedence at Sea, "The Liberty."

70. Major John Brown to General Montgomery, August 23, 1775.

71. Information Communicated to General Montgomery by Peter Griffin, August 25, 1775.

72. Randall, *Benedict Arnold*, 142.

73. Extract of Another Letter from Quebec, October 1, 1775.

74. Allen, *History of the State of Vermont*, 47.

75. Extract of Another Letter from Quebec, October 1, 1775.

76. General Schuyler to General Washington, August 31, 1775.

77. *Papers of George Washington*, "Phillip Schuyler, Letter to George Washington," August 6, 1775.

78. Millard, *Lake Passages*, 86.

79. Charbonneau, *Fortifications of Île Aux Noix*, 67.

80. Millard, *Lake Passages*, 87.

81. Fay, *Vermont's Ebenezer Allen*, 8, 46.

82. Hazen, February 17, 1776.

83. "Report on Simon Metcalf: 10 [December] 1782."

84. Millard, *Lake Passages*, 88.

85. Cubbison, *American Northern Theater Army*, 20.

86. Ibid., 22.

87. Jacob Bayley to Colonel Little, November 24, 1775.

Chapter 4

88. Cubbison, *American Northern Theater Army*, 21.

89. Schuyler to President of Congress, January 29, 1776.

90. Cubbison, *American Northern Theater Army*, 9.

91. Ibid., 34.

92. Ibid., 39.

93. Schuyler to President of Congress, January 29, 1776.

94. *Papers of George Washington*, "George Washington to Timothy Bidel," February 1, 1776.

95. Letter from General Wooster to Colonel Bayley, February 10, 1776.

96. Vermont Historical Society, "Colonel Frye Bailey's Reminiscences."

97. *Papers of George Washington*, "Bayley to Washington," April 15, 1776.

98. Charbonneau, *Fortifications of Île Aux Noix*, 77.

99. Cubbison, *American Northern Theater Army*, 41.

100. Ibid., 46.

101. Ibid., 48.

102. Ibid., 45.

103. Ibid., 23.

104. Ibid., 57.

105. Ibid., 57.

106. Ibid., 14.

107. Ibid., 16.

108. Ibid., 60.

109. Ibid.

110. Ibid., 66.

111. Letter from Colonel Bedel to the New-Hampshire Committee of Safety, March 8, 1776.

112. Vermont Historical Society, "Colonel Frye Bailey's Reminiscences."

113. *Papers of George Washington,*, "Bayley to Washington," April 15, 1776.

114. *Papers of George Washington*, "From George Washington to Samuel Adams," March 22, 1776.

115. Cubbison, *American Northern Theater Army*, 23.

116. Ibid., 65.

117. Ibid., 19.

118. Ibid., 106.

119. Ibid., 67.

120. *Papers of George Washington*, "Bayley to Washington," April 15, 1776.

121. Cubbison, *American Northern Theater Army*, 31.

122. Ibid., 68.

123. Ibid., 33.

124. *Papers of George Washington*, "Bayley to Washington," April 15, 1776.

125. Millard, *Lake Passages*, 99.

126. Everest, *Point Au Fer on Lake Champlain*, 18.

127. Ibid.

128. Cubbison, *American Northern Theater Army*, 86.

129. Ibid.

130. *Papers of George Washington*, "Washington to Bayley," April 29, 1776.

131. Randall, *Benedict Arnold*, 231.

132. Cubbison, *American Northern Theater Army*, 81.

133. Randall, *Benedict Arnold*, 229.

134. Cubbison, *American Northern Theater Army*, 14.

135. *Papers of George Washington*, "From George Washington to John Hancock," May 5, 1776.

136. Cubbison, *American Northern Theater Army*, 86.

137. Ibid., 89.

138. Ibid., 102.

139. Ibid., 109.

140. Millard, *Lake Passages*, 96.

141. Cubbison, *American Northern Theater Army*, 23.

142. Randall, *Benedict Arnold*, 236.

143. Cubbison, *American Northern Theater Army*, 23.

144. Millard, *Lake Passages*, 98.

145. Cubbison, *American Northern Theater Army*, 24.

146. Ibid., 100.

147. Ibid., 87.

148. Millard, *Lake Passages*, 101.

149. Everest, *Point Au Fer on Lake Champlain*, 19.

150. Letter from S. Metcalf to Colonel Jacob Bayley, July 21, 1776.

151. Enys, *American Journals of John Enys*.

152. Millard, *Lake Passages*, 101.

153. Enys, *American Journals of John Enys*.

154. Ibid.

155. Cubbison, *American Northern Theater Army*, 122.

156. Ibid., 124.

157. Millard, *Lake Passages*, 105.

158. Cubbison, *American Northern Theater Army*, 123.

159. General Schuyler to President of Congress, January 29, 1776.

160. Millard, *Lake Passages*, 107.

161. Cubbison, *American Northern Theater Army*, 124.

162. Ibid., 125.

163. Ibid., 127.

164. Ibid.

165. Millard, *Lake Passages*, 107.

166. Enys, *American Journals of John Enys*.

167. Millard, *Lake Passages*, 108.

Chapter 5

168. Cubbison, *American Northern Theater Army*, 128.

169. Millard, *Lake Passages*, 108.

170. Letter from General Sullivan to General Schuyler, June 24, 1776.

171. Letter from Colonel Hartley to General Gates, June 1776.

172. Everest, *Point Au Fer on Lake Champlain*, 20.

173. Extract of a Letter from Crown Point, July 3, 1776.

174. Letter from Charles Cushing to His Brother, July 8, 1776.

175. *Papers of George Washington*, "Washington to Bayley," June 25, 1776.

176. Cubbison, *American Northern Theater Army*, 129.

177. Ibid.

178. Fisher, "Loyalists of Strafford," 336.

179. Fay, *Vermont's Ebenezer Allen*, 8, 47.

180. Letter from General Washington to Colonel Bayley, June 25, 1776.

181. Kirkland, "Journal of a Physician," 338.

182. Simon Metcalf to Congress, 1782.

183. Letter from S. Metcalf to Colonel Jacob Bayley, July 21, 1776.

184. Letter from General Sullivan to the President of Congress, July 6, 1776.

185. Millard, *Lake Passages*, 111.

186. Cubbison, *American Northern Theater Army*, 131.

187. Millard, *Lake Passages*, 112.

188. Letter from S. Metcalf to Colonel Jacob Bayley, July 21, 1776.

189. Brownson, 1776.

190. Cubbison, *American Northern Theater Army*, 135.

191. Kirkland, "Journal of a Physician."

192. Charbonneau, *Fortifications of Île Aux Noix*, 78.

193. Sullivan 1776.

194. Haslam and Haslam, *Greensboro Blockhouse Project*, 24.

195. Ibid., 53.

196. Weare 1776.

197. Schenawolf, "Forgotten Warriors," 2019.

198. Colonel Hurd, August 8, 1776.

199. Everest, *Point Au Fer on Lake Champlain*, 20.

200. Letter from S. Metcalf to Colonel Jacob Bayley, July 21, 1776.

201. Letter from Captain Wilson to General Arnold, July 22, 1776.

202. Letter from Colonel Hartley to General Gates, July 24, 1776.

203. Enys, *American Journals of John Enys*.

204. Millard, *Lake Passages*, 119.

205. Letter from Colonel Hurd to the New-Hampshire Committee of Safety, July 27, 1776.

206. Letter from Jacob Bayley and James Bayley to General Gates, July 29, 1776.

207. Letter from General Gates to General Washington, July 29, 1776.

208. Daniel Hall, August 5, 1775.

209. Letter from Colonel Hurd to the New-Hampshire Committee of Safety, August 3, 1776.

210. Examination of Two Canadian Captains, August 6, 1776.

211. Millard, *Lake Passages*, 118.

212. Certificate of Lieutenant-Colonel Wait of the most advantageous post on Onion river, September 1, 1776.

213. Perry, *History of the Town of Swanton*, 968, 969.

214. Ibid., 970, 971.

215. National Archives, November 1776.

216. Ibid., 1782.

217. Millard, *Lake Passages*, 120.

218. Meshech Weare to Colonel Jacob Bayley, July 18, 1776.

219. Letter from Colonel Hartley to General Gates, August 11, 1776.

220. Letter from Jacob Bayley to General Gates, August 13, 1776.

221. Letter from Colonel Hartley to General Gates, August 11, 1776.

222. Millard, *Lake Passages*, 121.

223. Ibid., 123.

224. Charbonneau, *Fortifications of Île Aux Noix*, 81.

225. Ibid., 78.

226. Letter from Lieutenant-Colonel Brown to General Schuyler, August 27, 1776.

227. Examination of Antoine Girard, a Canadian, September 20, 1776.

228. Letter from Colonel Hurd to the New-Hampshire Committee of Safety, September 24, 1776.
229. Certificate of Lieutenant-Colonel Wait of the most advantageous post on Onion river, September 1, 1776.
230. Major John Brown to Governour Trumbull, August 14, 1775.
231. Enys, *American Journals of John Enys*.
232. Ibid.
233. Charbonneau, *Fortifications of Île Aux Noix*, 82.
234. Kelly, *Valcour*, 101.
235. Ibid., 102, 103.
236. Millard, *Lake Passages*, 124, 125.
237. Kelly, *Valcour*, 102,103.
238. Millard, *Lake Passages*, 127.
239. Kelly, *Valcour*, 104.
240. Information given by a Hessian deserter, September 5, 1776..
241. Millard, *Lake Passages*, 126.
242. Extract of a Letter from Crown Point: Account of the retreat of the Army from Sorel. July 3, 1776.
243. Letter from General Arnold to General Gates, September 9, 1776.
244. Kelly, *Valcour*, 105.
245. Ibid., 106.
246. Examination of Antoine Girard, a Canadian, September 20, 1776.
247. Letter from General Arnold to General Gates: Cannot but think it extremely cruel, September 15, 1776.
248. Kelly, *Valcour*, 112.
249. Letter from General Arnold to General Gates, September 9, 1776.
250. Kelly, *Valcour*, 112.
251. Millard, *Lake Passages*, 128.
252. Kelly, *Valcour*, 110.
253. Charbonneau, *Fortifications of Île Aux Noix*, 81.

Chapter 6

254. Kelly, *Valcour*, 133.
255. Ibid., 137.
256. Colonel Hurd, August 8, 1776.
257. Letter from General Arnold to General Gates, September 28, 1776.
258. Millard, *Lake Passages*, 130.

259. Kelly, *Valcour*, 112.
260. Examination of Sergeant Stiles, October 1, 1776.
261. Kelly, *Valcour*, 141.
262. Millard, *Lake Passages*, 131.
263. Ibid., 133.
264. Kelly, *Valcour*, 142.
265. Millard, *Lake Passages*, 133.
266. Fay, *Vermont's Ebenezer Allen*, 106.
267. Everest, *Point Au Fer on Lake Champlain*, 22.
268. Millard, *Lake Passages*, 149.
269. Ibid., 152.
270. Fisher, "Loyalists of Strafford," 335.

Chapter 7

271. Everest, *Point Au Fer on Lake Champlain*, 22.
272. Ibid., 22.
273. Millard, *Lake Passages*, 161.
274. Underwood, "Indian and Tory Raids," 207.
275. Millard, *Lake Passages*, 165.
276. Ibid., 167.
277. Everest, *Point Au Fer on Lake Champlain*, 22.
278. Millard, *Lake Passages*, 173.
279. Everest, *Point Au Fer on Lake Champlain*, 22.
280. Cubbison, *American Northern Theater Army*, 85.
281. Millard, *Lake Passages*, 179.

Chapter 8

282. Underwood, "Indian and Tory Raids."
283. Ibid., 202.
284. Nye, "Loayalists and Their Property," 33–44.
285. Fisher, "Loyalists of Strafford," 337.
286. Huden, "Colonel Thomas Johnson Papers and Documents," 92.
287. Fay, *Vermont's Ebenezer Allen*, 93.
288. Underwood, "Indian and Tory Raids," 204.
289. Metcalf, "Petition of Simon Metcalf," November 1777.

290. Vermont Historical Society, "Colonel Frye Bailey's Reminiscences."

Chapter 9

291. Charbonneau, *Fortifications of Île Aux Noix*, 33.
292. Ibid., 93.
293. Ibid., 71.
294. Everest, *Point Au Fer on Lake Champlain*, 26.
295. Gauthier, *Siege of the Moses Pierson Blockhouse*.
296. Allen, *History of the State of Vermont*, 74, 75.
297. Underwood, "Indian and Tory Raids," 209.
298. Fay, *Vermont's Ebenezer Allen*, 109.
299. Everest, *Point Au Fer on Lake Champlain*, 25.
300. Underwood, "Indian and Tory Raids," 205.
301. Ibid., 209.
302. Everest, *Point Au Fer on Lake Champlain*, 25.
303. Charbonneau, *Fortifications of Île Aux Noix*, 78 and 79.
304. Millard, *Lake Passages*, 201.
305. Brymner, *Report on Canadian Archives*, 908.
306. Enys, *American Journals of John Enys*.
307. Allen, *History of the State of Vermont*, 75.
308. Everest, *Point Au Fer on Lake Champlain*, 26.
309. Enys, *American Journals of John Enys*.
310. Ibid.
311. Ibid.
312. Ibid.
313. Ibid.
314. Ibid.
315. Underwood, "Indian and Tory Raids," 209.
316. Enys, *American Journals of John Enys*.
317. Fay, *Vermont's Ebenezer Allen*, 109.
318. Enys, *American Journals of John Enys*, 28, 29.
319. Ibid.
320. Ibid.
321. Millard, *Lake Passages*, 203.
322. Hemenway, *Vermont Historical Gazeteer*, 290.
323. Enys, *American Journals of John Enys*, 33.

Chapter 10

324. Enys, *American Journals of John Enys*, 34.
325. Brymner, *Report on Canadian Archives*, 169.
326. Ibid., 908.
327. Underwood, "Indian and Tory Raids," 205.
328. Allen, *History of the State of Vermont*, 77.
329. *Papers of George Washington*, "Schuyler to Washington," 1779.
330. Haslam and Haslam, *Greensboro Blockhouse Project*, 25.
331. Everest, *Point Au Fer on Lake Champlain*, 25.
332. Haslam and Haslam, *Greensboro Blockhouse Project*, 56.
333. Underwood, "Indian and Tory Raids," 205.
334. Ibid., 209.
335. Brymner, *Report on Canadian Archives*, 489.
336. Ibid., 173.
337. Ibid., 343.
338. Ibid., 370.
339. Ibid., 344.
340. Haslam and Haslam, *Greensboro Blockhouse Project*, 60.
341. Fay, *Vermont's Ebenezer Allen*, 119.
342. Brymner, *Report on Canadian Archives*, 908.
343. Haslam and Haslam, *Greensboro Blockhouse Project*, 26.
344. Underwood, "Indian and Tory Raids," 209.
345. Brymner, *Report on Canadian Archives*, 131.
346. Enys, *American Journals of John Enys*, 34.
347. Goodrich, *Rolls of the Soldiers*, 732.
348. Underwood, "Indian and Tory Raids," 212.

Chapter 11

349. Enys, *American Journals of John Enys*, 34.
350. *Papers of George Washington*, "To George Washington from Phillip Schuyler," January 16, 1780.
351. Geraw, *Enosburgh, Vermont*.
352. Underwood, "Indian and Tory Raids," 216.
353. Ibid., 218.
354. Hemenway, *Vermont Historical Gazeteer*, 359.
355. Allen, *History of the State of Vermont*, 94, 95.

356. Ibid., 104.
357. Brymner, *Report on Canadian Archives*, 349.
358. Goodrich, *Rolls of the Soldiers*, 732.
359. Brymner, *Report on Canadian Archives*, 179.
360. Underwood, "Indian and Tory Raids," 218.
361. Ibid., 219.
362. Fay, *Vermont's Ebenezer Allen*, 110.
363. Enys, *American Journals of John Enys*, 35.
364. Ibid.
365. Goodwin, "Narrative of a Captive," 116.
366. Enys, *American Journals of John Enys*, 36.
367. Ibid., 37.
368. Bennet, "Ethan Allen Homestead."
369. Enys, *American Journals of John Enys*, 48.
370. Fay, *Vermont's Ebenezer Allen*, 68.
371. Millard, *Lake Passages*, 203.
372. Goodwin, "Narrative of a Captive," 124.
373. Millard, *Lake Passages*, 203.
374. Enys, *American Journals of John Enys*, 49.
375. Fay, *Vermont's Ebenezer Allen*, 115.
376. Enys, *American Journals of John Enys*, 51.
377. Brymner, *Report on Canadian Archives*, 908.
378. Underwood, "Indian and Tory Raids," 209.
379. Fay, *Vermont's Ebenezer Allen*, 115.
380. Allen, *History of the State of Vermont*, 95.
381. Bennet, "Ethan Allen Homestead."
382. Allen, *History of the State of Vermont*, 96.
383. Brymner, *Report on Canadian Archives*, 908.
384. Ibid.

Chapter 12

385. Metcalf, "Simon Metcalf's 'Little Book.'"
386. Millard, *Lake Passages*, 204.
387. Allen, *History of the State of Vermont*, 96.
388. Goodrich, *Rolls of the Soldiers*, 725.
389. Underwood, "Indian and Tory Raids," 209.
390. Fay, *Vermont's Ebenezer Allen*, 110, 111.

391. Huden, "Colonel Thomas Johnson Papers and Documents," 95.

392. Metcalf, "Simon Metcalf's 'Little Book,'" 29.

393. Allen, *History of the State of Vermont*, 105.

394. Huden, "Colonel Thomas Johnson Papers and Documents," 95.

395. Underwood, "Indian and Tory Raids," 220.

396. Brymner, *Report on Canadian Archives*, 183.

397. Underwood, "Indian and Tory Raids," 220.

398. Brymner, *Report on Canadian Archives*, 358.

399. Ibid., 909.

400. Millard, *Lake Passages*, 204.

401. Allen, *History of the State of Vermont*, 108.

402. Brymner, *Report on Canadian Archives*, 181.

403. Ibid., 361.

404. Ibid., 909.

405. Everest, *Point Au Fer on Lake Champlain*, 26.

406. Brymner, *Report on Canadian Archives*, 378.

407. Goodrich, *Rolls of the Soldiers*, 732.

408. Brymner, *Report on Canadian Archives*, 910.

409. Ibid., 361.

410. Bennet, "Ethan Allen Homestead."

411. Brymner, *Report on Canadian Archives*, 910.

412. Ibid., 379.

413. Ibid., 910.

414. Allen, *History of the State of Vermont*, 113.

415. Huden, "Colonel Thomas Johnson Papers and Documents," 115.

416. Enys, *American Journals of John Enys*, 53.

Chapter 13

417. Brymner, *Report on Canadian Archives*, 393.

418. Everest, *Point Au Fer on Lake Champlain*, 28.

419. Metcalf, "Simon Metcalf's 'Little Book,'" 29.

420. Bennet, "Ethan Allen Homestead."

421. Allen, *History of the State of Vermont*, 144.

422. Brymner, *Report on Canadian Archives*, 395.

423. Charbonneau, *Fortifications of Île Aux Noix*, 75.

424. Huden, "Colonel Thomas Johnson Papers and Documents," 109.

425. Brymner, *Report on Canadian Archives*, 380.
426. Huden, "Colonel Thomas Johnson Papers and Documents," 115.
427. Goodwin, "Narrative of a Captive," 136.
428. "Report on Simon Metcalf: 10 [December] 1782."
429. Metcalf, "Simon Metcalf's 'Little Book,'" 31.
430. Everest, *Point Au Fer on Lake Champlain*, 28.
431. Charbonneau, *Fortifications of Île Aux Noix*, 95.
432. Riedesel, *Baroness von Riedesel and the American Revolution*, 125.
433. Brymner, *Report on Canadian Archives*, 456.
434. Everest, *Point Au Fer on Lake Champlain*, 28.
435. Riedesel, *Baroness von Riedesel and the American Revolution*, 210.
436. Brymner, *Report on Canadian Archives*, 417.
437. Millard, *Lake Passages*, 203.
438. Hemenway, *Vermont Historical Gazeteer*, 708.
439. Brymner, *Report on Canadian Archives*, 426.
440. Charbonneau, *Fortifications of Île Aux Noix*, 76.
441. Fay, *Vermont's Ebenezer Allen*, 125.
442. Everest, *Point Au Fer on Lake Champlain*, 32.
443. Charbonneau, *Fortifications of Île Aux Noix*, 93.
444. Ibid, 96
445. Millard, *Lake Passages*, 209.
446. Brymner, *Report on Canadian Archives*, 710, 844.
447. Millard, *Lake Passages*, 209.
448. Fay, *Vermont's Ebenezer Allen*, 129.
449. Brymner, *Report on Canadian Archives*, 714.
450. Fay, *Vermont's Ebenezer Allen*, 129.
451. Brymner, *Report on Canadian Archives*, 794.
452. Enys, *American Journals of John Enys*, 90.
453. Ibid., 91.
454. Millard, *Lake Passages*, 210.
455. Charbonneau, *Fortifications of Île Aux Noix*, 110.
456. Millard, *Lake Passages*, 211.
457. Fay, *Vermont's Ebenezer Allen*, 133.
458. Enys, *American Journals of John Enys*, 173.
459. Ibid.
460. Mayo, *Forty-Fifth Parallel*, 263.
461. Millard, *Lake Passages*, 211.
462. Everest, *Point Au Fer on Lake Champlain*, 36.

463. Charbonneau, *Fortifications of Île Aux Noix*, 113.
464. Everest, *Point Au Fer on Lake Champlain*, 40.
465. Millard, *Lake Passages*, 215.
466. Everest, *Point Au Fer on Lake Champlain*, 38.
467. Ibid., 41.

BIBLIOGRAPHY

Allen, Ira. *History of the State of Vermont*. Rutland, VT: Charles E. Tuttle Company, 1973.

American War for Indepedence at Sea. "The Liberty." Accessed August 8, 2021. https://www.awiatsea.com.

Bellico, Russell. *Journeys in War and Peace*. Fleischmann, NY: Purple Mountain Press, 1999.

———. *Sales and Steam in the Moutains*. Fleischmanns, NY: Purple Mountain Press, 1992.

Bennet, David. "Ethan Allen Homestead." March 15, 2015. Accessed December 23, 2021. https://ethanallenhomestead.org.

———. *A Few Lawless Vagabonds*. Philadelphia: Casemate, 2014.

Brymner, Douglas. *Report on Canadian Archives*. Ottowa: McClean, Roger, & Company, 1887.

Chamberlain, Silas. February 21, 1776. Accessed August 17, 2021. https://docs.google.com/document/d/1lQFHlagfSWmwITJK4RjnTJEna2EPOnQBvuvegLbvQxM/edit#heading=h.d2dmkxfiim5j.

Charbonneau, Andre. *The Fortifications of Île Aux Noix*. Ottawa: Canadian Heritage Parks Canada, 1994.

Cubbison, Douglas R. *The American Northern Theater Army in 1776*. Jefferson, NC: McFarland & Company, 2010.

Enys, John. *The American Journals of John Enys*. Edited by Elizabeth Cometti. Syracuse, NY: Syracuse University Press, 1976.

Everest, Allan S. *Point Au Fer on Lake Champlain*. Plattsburgh, NY: Clinton County Historical Association, 1992.

Fay, Glenn, Jr. *Vermont's Ebenezer Allen*. Charleston, SC: The History Press, 2021.

Fisher, Josephine. "Loyalists of Strafford." *Vermont Historical Society Journal* (1937): 335.

Freeman, S.A. *Documents of the Senate of the State of New York*. Vol. 5. Albany: Dental Society of the State of New York, 1877.

Gauthier, Brennan. *The Siege of the Moses Pierson Blockhouse*. Burlington, VT: Ethan Allen Homestead Presentation, September 9, 2019.

Geraw, Janice Fleury. *Enosburgh, Vermont*. Enosburgh, VT: Enosburgh Historical Society, 1985.

Goodrich, John E. *Rolls of the Soldiers in the Revolutionary War, 1775 to 1783*. Rutland: Vermont Historical Society, Tuttle Company, 1904.

Goodwin, Neil. "Narrative of a Captive, George Avery 1780–1782." *Journal of Vermont History* 80 (2012): 112–40.

Haslam, Jill Baker, and Patricia L. Haslam. *The Greensboro Blockhouse Project*. Daytona Beach, FL: Indiego Publishing, 2007.

Hemenway, Abby. *Vermont Historical Gazetteer*. Vol. 1. Burlington, VT: Abby Hemenway, 1867.

Huden, John C. *Indian Troubles in Early Vermont*. Vol. 25. Montpelier: Vermont Historical Society, 1957.

———. "Colonel Thomas Johnson Papers and Documents." *Vermont History Journal* (1923–25): 87–117.

Kelly, Jack. *Valcour: The 1776 Campaign That Saved the Cause of Liberty*. New York: St. Martin's Press, 2021.

Kirkland, Frederic R. 1935. "Journal of a Physician on the Expedition to Canada." *Pennsylvania Magazine* 59 (4): 321–61.

Lampee, Thomas. "The Missisquoi Loyalists." *Vermont Historical Journal* 6, no. 2 (1938).

Madison, James. "The Papers of James Madison." December 1782. Founders Online. National Archives. Chicago: University of Chicago.

Mayo, Lawrence. 1923. *The Forty-Fifth Parallel: A Detail of the Unguarded Boundary*. Edited by the American Geographical Society. Vol. 13. New York: Library of the University of California, Riverside.

Metcalf, Simon. "Petition of Simon Metcalf." National Archives UK. November 1777. Accessed August 27, 2021. https://discovery. nationalarchives.gov.uk/details/r/C9295975.

———. "Simon Metcalf's 'Little Book.'" *Bulletin of the Fort Ticonderoga Museum* (1988): 26–36.

Millard, James P. *Lake Passages, A Journey Through the Centuries*. South Hero, VT: America's Historic Lakes, 2007.

Myrick, Rawson C. Vermont Secretary of State. *State Papers of Vermont*. Montpellier: State of Vermont, 1947.

National Archives. November 1776. Accessed August 27, 2021. https://search.ancestry.com.

———. December 15, 1775. Accessed August 27, 2021. https://search.ancestry.com.

Nelson, James L. *Benedict Arnold's Navy*. Camden, ME: McGraw-Hill, 2006.

Nople, Henry Harmn. "Original Swanton Grant." *Montpelier Morning Journal*, August 17, 1910, 4.

Nye, Mary Greene. "Loyalists and Their Property." *Vermont Historical Society Journal* (1942): 36–44.

Palmer, Peter Sailly. *History of Lake Champlain*. Albany, NY: J. Munsell, 1853.

The Papers of George Washington. "Bayley to Washington." April 15, 1776. Founders Online. National Archives. Charlottesville: University Press of Virginia.

———. "From George Washington to John Hancock." May 5, 1776. Founders Online. National Archives. Charlottesville: University Press of Virginia.

———. "From George Washington to Samuel Adams." March 22, 1776. Founders Online. National Archives. Charlottesville, VA: University Press of Virginia.

———. "From Washington to Colonel Jacob Bayley." October 7, 1776. Founders Online. Charlottesville: University Press of Virginia.

———. "George Washington to Timothy Bidel." February 1, 1776. Founders Online. National Archives. Charlottesville: University Press of Virginia.

———. "Phillip Schuyler, Letter to George Washington." August 6, 1775. Founders Online. National Archives. Charlottesville: University Press of Virginia.

———. "Schuyler to Washington." March 1, 1779. Founders Online. National Archives. Charlottesville: University of Virginia Press.

———. "To George Washington from Jacob Bayley." February 26, 1776. Founders Online. National Archives. Charlottesville: University Press of Virginia,

———. "To George Washington from Phillip Schuyler." January 16, 1780. Founders Online. National Archives. Charlottesville: University of Virginia Press.

———. "Washington to Bayley." June 25, 1776. Founders Online. National Archives. Charlottesville, VA: University Press of Virginia.

———. "Washington to Bayley." April 29, 1776. Founders Online. National Archives. Charlottesville, VA: University Press of Virginia.

Perry, Barney. *History of the Town of Swanton.* Swanton, VT: Abbey Hemenway, 1882.

Randall, Willard. *Benedict Arnold, Patriot and Traitor.* New York: William Morrow & Company, 1990.

———. *Ethan Allen: His Life and Times.* New York: W.W. Norton and Company, 2011.

"Report on Simon Metcalf: 10 [December] 1782." Founders Online. National Archives. Accessed August 10, 2021.

Riedesel, Baroness von. 1965. *Baroness von Riedesel and the American Revolution.* Kingsport, TN: Kingsport Press.

Schenawolf, Harry. "Forgotten Warriors of the American Revolution: Major Benjamin Whitcomb of 'Whitcomb's Raiders.'" *Revolutionary War Journal.* June 10, 2019. Accessed August 1, 2021. https://www.revolutionarywarjournal.com.

Shattuck, Gary. *The Rebel and the Tory.* Barre: Vermont Historical Society, 2020.

Underwood, Wynn. "Indian and Tory Raids on the Otter Valley, 1777–1782." *Vermont Quarterly* (1947): 195–221.

Vermont Historical Society. "Colonel Frye Bailey's Reminiscences." *Vermont History Journal* (1923–25): 22–45.

Wells, Bayze. Journal of 1775. "Orderly Book and Journals Kept by Connecticut Men While Taking Part in the American Revolution. 1775–1778." *Connecticut Historical Society* (1889): 232–48. Accessed August 7, 2021.

Northern Illinois University Digital Library (https://digital.lib.niu.edu)

Abstract of Lieutenant Benjamin Whitcomb's Report. Accessed August 21, 2021.

An Account of the Voyage of Captain Remember Baker. July 26, 1775. Accessed August 7, 2021.

Captain Johnson's Notes of a Road from Newbury to St. Johns. March 26 and April 9, 1776. Accessed August 18, 2021.

Certificate of Lieutenant-Colonel Wait of the most advantageous post on Onion river. September 1, 1776. Accessed August 21, 2021.

Colonel Hurd. August 8, 1776. Accessed August 20, 2021.

Daniel Hall. August 5, 1775. Accessed August 20, 2021.

Deposition of John Duguid. August 2, 1775. Accessed August 7, 2021.

Deposition of John Shatforth. August 2, 1775. Accessed August 7, 2021.

Examination of Antoine Girard, a Canadian. September 20, 1776. Accessed August 21, 2021.

Examination of Sergeant Stiles. October 1, 1776. Accessed August 21, 2021.

Examination of Two Canadian Captains. August 6, 1776. Accessed August 20, 2021.

Extract of Another Letter from Quebec. October 1, 1775. Accessed August 9, 2021

Extract of a Letter from Crown Point: Account of the retreat of the Army from Sorel. July 3, 1776. Accessed August 19, 2021.

General Schuyler to the Continental Congress. July 27, 1775. Accessed August 7, 2021.

General Schuyler to General Washington. August 31, 1775. Accessed August 9, 2021.

General Schuyler to General Washington. September 20, 1775. Accessed August 10, 2021.

General Schuyler to President of Congress. January 29, 1776. Accessed August 17, 2021.

Hazen. February 17, 1776. Accessed August 10, 2021.

Information Communicated to General Montgomery by Peter Griffin. August 25, 1775. Accessed August 8, 2021.

Information given by a Hessian deserter. September 5, 1776. Accessed August 21, 2021.

Intelligence at Exeter, New-Hampshire, from Onion river, of houses being destroyed by British troops. September 7, 1776. Accessed August 20, 2021.

Jacob Bayley to Colonel Little. November 24, 1775. Accessed August 11, 2021.

Letter from Captain Brownson to General Gates. August 11, 1776. Accessed February 27, 2021.

Letter from Captain Brownson to General Gates. July 14, 1776. Accessed February 27, 2021.

Letter from Captain Wilson to General Arnold. July 22, 1776. Accessed August 20, 2021.

Letter from Charles Cushing to his Brother. July 8, 1776. Accessed August 19, 2021.

Letter from Colonel Bayley to Colonel Hurd: Intelligence from Canada, brought by Sergeant Daniel Booth, a deserter. September 24, 1776. Accessed August 21, 2021.

Letter from Colonel Bedel to the New-Hampshire Committee of Safety. March 8, 1776. Accessed August 17, 2021.

Letter from Colonel Hartley to General Gates. July 24, 1776. Accessed August 20, 2021.

Letter from Colonel Hartley to General Gates. July 30, 1776. Accessed August 20, 2021.

Letter from Colonel Hartley to General Gates. August 11, 1776. Accessed August 20, 2021.

Letter from Colonel Hurd to General Sullivan. July 13, 1776. Accessed August 19, 2021.

Letter from Colonel Hurd to the New-Hampshire Committee of Safety. July 27, 1776. Accessed August 20, 2021.

Letter from Colonel Hurd to the New-Hampshire Committee of Safety. August 3, 1776. Accessed August 20, 2021.

Letter from Colonel Wait to Colonel Hurd. July 20, 1776. Accessed August 20, 2021.

Letter from General Arnold to General Gates. Accessed August 21, 2021.

Letter from General Arnold to General Gates. September 9, 1776. Accessed August 21, 2021.

Letter from General Arnold to General Gates. September 28, 1776. Accessed August 21, 2021.

Letter from General Arnold to General Gates: Cannot but think it extremely cruel, when he has sacrificed ease.... September 15, 1776. Accessed August 21, 2021.

Letter from General Gates to General Washington. July 29, 1776. Accessed August 20, 2021.

Letter from General Schuyler to Meshech Weare: The troops from New-Hampshire for Canada are to march by the most direct road to Onion River or to Crown Point. June 18, 1776. Accessed August 18, 2021.

Letter from General Schuyler to the President of Congress. January 10, 1776. Accessed August 17, 2021.

Letter from General Sullivan to General Schuyler. June 24, 1776. Accessed August 19, 2021.

Letter from General Sullivan to the President of Congress. July 6, 1776. Accessed August 19, 2021.

Letter from General Washington to Colonel Bayley. June 25, 1776. Accessed August 19, 2021.

Letter from General Washington to the President of Congress. May 5, 1776. Accessed August 18, 2021.

Letter from General Wooster to Colonel Bayley. February 10, 1776. Accessed August 17, 2021.

Letter from Jacob Bayley to General Gates. August 13, 1776. Accessed August 20, 2021.

Letter from Jacob Bayley and James Bayley to General Gates. July 29, 1776. Accessed August 20, 2021.

Letter from Lieutenant-Colonel Brown to General Schuyler. August 27, 1776. Accessed August 20, 2021.

Letter from S. Metcalf to Colonel Jacob Bayley. July 21, 1776. Accessed August 19, 2021.

Major John Brown to General Montgomery. August 23, 1775. Accessed August 8, 2021.

Major John Brown to Governour Trumbull. August 14, 1775. Accessed August 7, 2021.

Meshech Weare to Colonel Jacob Bayley. July 18, 1776. Accessed August 20, 2021.

Order to Commanding Officer of the Company raised by Captain Faucett to maintain his post at Jerico, on Onion River. September 1, 1776. Accessed August 20, 2021.

Paper delivered Major-General Schuyler by Captain Smith. August 2, 1775. Accessed August 7, 2021.

Petition. Continental Congress. June 28, 1776. Accessed August 19, 2021.

Petition of the inhabitants of Onion River. August 6, 1776. Accessed August 20, 2021.

Report of Jas. Stewart. August 3, 1775. Accessed August 7, 2021.

INDEX

ABOUT THE AUTHOR

Jason Barney lives in St. Albans, Vermont. He is married to Christine Eldred and has a teenage son, Sam. They share a beautiful old farmhouse with two cats, Fiona and Wiggles. He has published approximately one hundred short stories with various small presses. He has written two prior books, *Northern Vermont in the War of 1812* and *The Hidden History of Franklin County, Vermont*, both published by The History Press. Jason is a science-fiction nerd and maintains the Star Trek timeline for Pocket Books.

He has been teaching at Missisquoi Valley Union High School for nineteen years. He has received the local VFW Teacher of the Year award and was awarded the Vermont Humanities Victor R. Swenson Award in 2019. In the summer of 2021, he was a co-director of a National Endowment for the Humanities Council Grant with the Vermont Archaeological Society. In the fall of 2021, he was the Missisquoi Valley Union Teacher of the Year.

Jason is forty-six years old.

Visit us at
www.historypress.com